T0078389

# THE
# ALTERNATIVE
# PLAN

## RENEGADE RESTORED
## TESTIMONY OF A BACKSLIDER

### Expanded Edition

No matter how many mistakes you have made or how far you have
walked away from the Lord, God has not changed His plans for you.
God can still realign your life to fit the plan He intended for you.

## Pauline Adongo

WESTBOW
PRESS®
A DIVISION OF THOMAS NELSON
& ZONDERVAN

# CONTENTS

# DEDICATION

I dedicate this book to the Lord God Almighty, Who redeemed me and appointed me to be a co-heir with my Lord Jesus Christ. God restored me to Himself out of His loving-kindness and mercy. The Lord Who values me will make certain I accomplish the marvelous plans He has for me. The Lord has pursued me relentlessly in love and compassion. Thank you, Lord, for Your reckless and relentless love. Thank You, Father, for restoration, deliverance, and healing. I exalt You, Lord. I am committed to serving you with all my heart, henceforth. To You be all glory, honor, adoration, and power forever. Amen!

# BOOK COVER

# THE STORY OF THE WHITE LILY

I wrote the original edition of this book, which was also my first book, in 2015, six years after rededicating my life to Christ. I have always loved writing. English and history were my favorite subjects when I was in middle school, also called primary school in Africa and high school. I always loved to participate in debate clubs, write English compositions, and read novels. I envisioned myself using laptops to express my thoughts back in the early nineties before laptops were available. In college, My essays were handwritten since English courses were prerequisites for my major. I am so glad we have since transitioned from Brother typewriters to desktop computers to laptops and tablets. Praise God for technology!

As any new author would attest, much effort goes into writing and publishing a book. The cover design is an integral part of this process. A book cover should tell a story to the reader just by its design. I was new to this process, so I struggled with what the cover for this first book should be. I did not receive an idea for the cover until I was about to submit the manuscript for publication. I use the word "receive" because that is what happened. One night I tossed and turned in bed until around four or five in the morning when I saw a detailed vision of the book cover. I could visualize the dark blue background of the cover with a large white flower, facing upwards! I had seen that species of flowers before. My neighbors had yellow versions of it in their front yard, and though I frequently admired my neighbor's flowers, I did not know what they were called.

Later that day, I conducted a Google search of white flower images. Guess what? The results showed the exact image I had seen in the vision. The flower was a large White Trumpet Lily! In the vision, I had seen golden pollen emitting from the delicate internal parts of the blossom, splattering in the air and on the pedals, which exactly matched the Google image! Praise God for Google Search! In my naivety, I did not connect the symbolism of the golden pollen until later, after the book was published. A co-worker who purchased the book commented on the cover, saying, "Pauline, the cover is a white lily; do you know that lilies can thrive in murky places, but they are always radiant?" Of course, the light bulb lit up in my head, and I decided to explore the meaning of white Lilies (or lilies in general) and the possible significance of the dark navy-blue background. God speaks through colors and other parts of His creation, but back then, I was clueless of the many ways God communicates with His people.

There are several metaphoric applications of a white trumpet lily. A [1]Lily stands for love; it embodies the purity of Jesus Christ. Lilies grow in secret hidden places; a lily also represents lips that speak sweet fragranced words, and lastly, a lily speaks of being clothed in spiritual glory. The sum of these descriptions is an accurate illustration of my testimony and my purpose in writing this book. Jesus accepted me as a prodigal, preparing me in hiding for nine months. I experienced the love of God during that incubation process, through which He birthed this book. I hope that as you read this book, you will reflect on the endless love of God and gain some insight into how He sees you. His love brings back rebels like me, who had forsaken His ways. God loves us no matter what condition we are in; there

---

[1] (Beale, 2011) Beale, Adam F. Thomson, Adrian. *The Divinity Code, Understanding Your Dreams and Visions* (2011)

is nothing we can do to influence Him to love us more or love us less. He still wants to nurture us privately, as He did with me, to mold us into vessels that will radiate His glory on earth.

In the vision, the trumpet lily faced upwards; this is a picture of believers' confidence as we walk courageously and hold our heads up as overcomers. Embrace the journey, and the Lord will walk with you as you read this book. Consider that, like a lily hidden in the Lord's bosom, you will experience transformation as you gaze into His eyes. Paul writes, *"we, with unveiled face, beholding as in a mirror the glory of the Lord, are being transformed into the same image from glory to glory, just as by the Spirit of the Lord." 2 Corinthians 3:18 NKJV.* Enjoy your transformation process as you read along.

[2]The color white stands for righteousness, like the pure, holy garments of a believer who has been washed clean and purified. White also characterizes innocence like an angel, symbolizes a field ready for harvest, a glory cloud, or glory as in the phrase, "whiter-than-snow," victorious, or full of light. I consider white to be the color of the redeeming grace of the Lord. Despite the filthiness of my backslidden condition, I discovered that God desires all of His children to enjoy eternity with Him. *The Lord is not slow about His promise, as some count slowness, but is patient toward you, not wishing for any to perish but for all to come to repentance, 2 Peter 3:9 NIV.* Repentance is a change in attitude, meaning to turn around and walk the other way. Repentance draws us to God, not away from Him. Romans 2:4-5 TPT says, do the riches of his extraordinary kindness make you take him for granted and despise him? Haven't you experienced how kind and understanding he has been to you? Do not mistake his tolerance for acceptance. **Do you realize that all the wealth of his extravagant kindness is meant to melt your heart and lead you into repentance? But because of your calloused**

[2] (Beale, 2011) Beale, Adam F. Thomson, Adrian. *The Divinity Code, Understanding Your Dreams and Visions* (2011)

**heart and refusal to change direction,** you are piling up wrath for yourself in the day of wrath when God's righteous judgment is revealed." Verse 5 speaks to the details I have shared about the backslidden life. God continues to amaze me!

Our celebration of eternity starts here on earth. There is no sin too huge that God cannot forgive. He promises to wash us as white as snow, and never remember our sins; God in this promise says. *I (God), even I, am He who blots out your transgressions, for My own sake, and remembers your sins no more," Isaiah 43:25 NIV.* Repentance qualifies us to attain righteousness. By the blood of Christ Jesus, we are made righteous, and our identity is restored as we are clothed in glory; then, we will desire to get to the harvest fields to bring others to share in that same glory.

The white lily sprouts from the main branch, reaching outward and releasing its pollen. That metaphor represents my journey out of the darkness to the restoration of my true identity. The Lord brought me out of murky places, forgave me, healed, delivered me, and is currently helping me blossom. This restoration will result in fruitfulness, as I press on to bear more seeds that can be disseminated to impact those around me and in distant places.

A lily's whiteness exceeds all whiteness. The flower's beauty and fragrance are attractive. A lily grows tall and strong, as much as 4-6 feet (120cm -180cm tall). Lilies also have medicinal value; lily oil is used for skincare. The white Lily represents the treasure God sees in each person. God yearns to see these treasures drawn from within us and brought to the surface to mature, to be productive, and to thrive. The white Lily represents people who may think they have gone beyond help, yet God still reaches down to restore them, inspiring them to blossom and resume the journey of their destinies. That white Lily represents you and me.

[3] The dark blue color represents the Holy Spirit. A regular blue color represents royalty, heavenly, spiritual, or healing as a complete heavenly reality. The color blue can be seen as a reminder to seek God's Kingdom or direction first. In the vision, the white lily was surrounded by a dark blue background, which denotes the environment in which we will thrive. That environment is the presence of the Holy Spirit.

Self-reliance and self-preservation were critical factors that drove my ambition in life. But there is nothing anyone can do successfully without the presence of the Lord, who is the Holy Spirit. He was sent to us by Jesus Christ as a Guide, Teacher, Advocate, and Intercessor; He is also the Breath of God (see John chapters 14 and 16). A life devoid of the Breath of God suffocates! This reminds me of the cry Moses made to God while leading the Israelites. Moses prayed, saying, *"now, therefore, I pray You, if I have found favor in Your sight, let me know Your ways that I may know You, so that I may find favor in Your sight. Consider, too, that this nation is Your people." And He said, "My presence shall go with you, and I will give you rest." Then he (Moses) said to Him (God), "If Your presence does not go with us, do not lead us up from here,"* Exodus 33:13-15 NASB. The dark-blue color on the cover is indicative of our continuous need to be covered by the Holy Spirit. Through Him, we can successfully fulfill our destinies here on earth.

---

[3] (Beale, 2011)-Beale, Adam F. Thomson, Adrian. *The Divinity Code, Understanding Your Dreams and Visions* (2011)

# INTRODUCTION

This is the story of my restoration to Jesus Christ after living a backslidden life. "Backslidden," (to backslide) is a term used mostly among born-again Christians. This term refers to a person who has reverted to a compromised lifestyle, contrary to the behavior of a fully submitted and committed Christian. There are two more definitions that so accurately describe my previous experience. One is [4] a backslider is a person who once had salvation but has since turned away from the Lord Jesus to the point that he or she is now spiritually lost and dead again, just like he or she was before becoming saved. Another definition is [5] a person who turned to crooked ways and strayed from the path of understanding (according to Proverbs 21:16). My definition of backsliding is to live a life that is not fully committed, loyal to God, living a life that seems to be occasionally committed but is mostly filled with compromise and lower moral standards. I fit all four definitions!

I expounded on some parts of my testimony, hoping that my story will inspire many to assess their current path and either stay committed to God or rededicate all areas of their lives to God. As you read, you will understand the reason for writing the new edition for this book.

The inception of this book began with a sermon that I wrote in November 2009. I experienced a significant setback when I lost my professional job in May of that year and remained jobless

---

[4] https://www.evangelicaloutreach.org/backslider.htm
[5] https://www.evangelicaloutreach.org/backslider.htm

for ten months. During that season, I spent most of my time in prayer, fasting, and devotion, as it was my first experience of such adversity. I did not know what to do other than seek God. On the other hand, however, I also knew that God was using the job loss to draw my attention. I had repeatedly ignored His promptings regarding my calling and my level of commitment to live a Christian life. During my unemployment, I continued to apply for jobs and go for interviews. Aside from the job search, I stayed mainly at home praying, listening to teachings from various ministers, fasting, and reading the Bible. Six months into this setback, I felt an urge to write sermons. I was not sure why, but neither did I fathom becoming a minister of the Gospel. I had always admired the ministers on television, even making comments like, "I think I could preach to audiences," but I was clueless about what the Lord was doing in me in 2009. So, one night in November 2009, I stayed up late writing a sermon titled, "The Alternative Plan." The sermon reflected the life I had lived up to that point. Before that night, I had written several sermons already; however, there was something different about this particular one. As I wrote, I kept receiving more revelation; I wrote from eleven at night to three in the morning. At one point, I recall asking the Holy Spirit to please let me go to sleep because I was so tired from writing. Upon that request, the revelation stopped!

That sermon, along with others, stayed dormant in my notebook until 2015 when I received a word of prophecy that "An Alternative Plan" was meant to be a book. I immediately had an epiphany and remembered why I could not stop writing that November night, as the Holy Spirit dictated the sermon. The Holy Spirit used the sermon to open my eyes to the realities of my life as a believer and the consequences of living a double life. I felt like I was being purged and shown the effects of my experience as a committed believer, contrasted with my life as a compromised believer.

The people I hope to influence are young adults who have just begun to venture in establishing their lives, and to immigrants whose faith in God was strong before they moved to a new country. These young-adults are just starting their independent life and are career-minded individuals. I acknowledge that what I write is sometimes raw and blunt. However, I desire that my vulnerability and transparency shed light on the potential pitfalls that can occur when someone tries to pursue a supposed destiny apart from God. The ability to attain ultimate success and fulfillment in any area of life is built upon God's foundation; see Psalm 127:1-2.

My goal is to encourage anyone who feels unsettled and is looking for fulfillment in life. I want to assure anyone who has backslidden or has lived a compromised lifestyle that God's plan for us will never change. No matter how much we have messed up, moved away from God, made mistakes or poor decisions, God has a great individualized plan laid out for each of us before we were born. The Apostle Paul says, *"for we are God's handiwork, His workmanship recreated in Christ Jesus, born anew that we may do those works which God predestined planned beforehand for us that we should walk in them," Ephesians 3:10, AMPC.* God's will and desire for each us to walk in and fulfill that predestined plan that He has for us. God did not design plans for failure, cycles of adversity, lack, sickness, stagnation, or misery. God desires for us to prosper in all things. God says *for I know the plans I have for you, says the Lord. They are plans for good and not for disaster, to give you a future and a hope, Jeremiah 29:11 NLT.* God has the perfect plan for life, health, prosperity, happiness, success, and fulfillment, and He is ever open to redirecting us to enjoy this plan! As you read this book, accept God's restorative grace, knowing that He receives us in any condition, and He wants to realign you with the intended plan He has for you.

# CHAPTER ONE

# THE QUEST TO OVERCOME MY PAST

I accepted Jesus Christ as Lord and Savior when I was twelve years old. My family, all six of us, lived in a one-room house in Pioneer Estate. We all became born again on the same night, through a brother named Kimani, in Eldoret, Kenya. My Mom overheard this brother ministering to our neighbor, and she then invited him to minister to us. Shortly afterward, we received ministry from a different pastor for the baptism of the Holy Spirit. That Saturday afternoon, our whole family was filled with the gifts of the Holy Spirit that were manifested by speaking in tongues and prophetic gifts that we came to learn of much later in adulthood. What a testimony! I remained an active believer in high school and through my relocation to the USA.

Interestingly, the poverty-stricken environment I grew up in did not hinder me from dreaming big. I grew up primarily in the slums of Kenya, namely Rhonda in Nakuru, Langas in Eldoret, and Nyalenda in Kisumu. Our family's one-roomed house was partitioned by a curtain to separate my Mom's sleeping quarters from ours. I had four siblings when I was twelve years old. Life to us seemed comfortable and normal. To date, I still thank my Mom for the sacrifices she made for us; she gave us her best as a single mother.

I felt obligated, as the eldest child, to help my mother and siblings. I realized that getting a good education was the only way out of poverty, so I determined to excel academically and professionally. I started playing "house" at a young age when I was about five years old. Playing House mimics the adult lifestyle in a fictional house. I manufactured imaginary parents, children, and conversations. Since I was the only child at that time, I was often tended by adults with whom I could not play, so my childhood playtime revolved around behaving like an adult and running my own "house." I spent much time in solitude, always picturing my future. Between five and twelve years old, my bedroom became my playroom. Most of my time, while I was playing house, I was busy planning out my future. I set academic and professional goals, accompanied by the timeframes for their accomplishment. The grace of God was there for me. I worked hard in school and completed my associate's and bachelor's degrees in my mid-twenties and my master's degree in my early thirties. Then the real quest to beat the odds started!

My ideal professional goal was to be a judge. I was fascinated by the law. I recall telling my eighth-grade teacher that I wanted to be a judge, and even now, I cannot forget her smile and enthusiasm. She urged me to go all-out in my pursuit. In my zeal, I later revealed my plans to a distant uncle, but he discouraged me by suggesting that judges send innocent people to jail. His response disturbed me; I did not want to accept the responsibility of sentencing someone from a possible wrongful conviction. I know now that my uncle was not a good confidant, but rather, a dream killer. I have since learned to use discernment before sharing my dreams.

My siblings and I have something unique in common: despite the challenges of living in the slums and being raised by a single mother, we never saw ourselves as deprived! This attitude continues to fascinate us today as adults, but I also know that God did not consider us as poor. We were in Christ, adopted into the family of God, and co-heirs with Christ. The Holy

Spirit helped each of us to press through the odds because of this attitude. God's favor and protection guided us as we prayed in faith. God also surrounded us with a supportive network of extended family members, namely, my maternal grandmother, aunts, and uncles.

My grandmother championed education. Despite her old age, she once visited me at my alma mater, a girls' boarding school in Home-Bay, Kenya. Grandma even paid my tuition for one semester. My aunts were instrumental in exposing my siblings and me to life outside the slums. Our first trip to the big city of Nairobi was to attend my uncle's wedding.

My aunts engineered further exposure to city life. One of my aunts was the first one to expose us to the world outside the slums. She was the first to introduce me to make up just before I turned twenty. Although we were accustomed to our home cities, visiting the capital city was the pinnacle of our dreams. My aunts and uncles were well accomplished. They were college graduates with high profile jobs in banking, information technology, accounting, and entrepreneurship. We looked up to them. When we visited them, we were inspired to work even more challengingly. All the adults in our family placed great emphasis on prayer, education, and etiquette. The saying was, if you did something wrong, grandma would know about it by the time you visited her in the village! My aunts served as personal coaches and mentors, while my uncles served as father figures since we were fatherless. We knew whom to go to when the need arose. I am sincerely thankful for the nurture and support of my family, including Grandma's sacrificial love.

Now, at this point, you might say, "Wow, Pauline, you had a lot going on there: you were first-born in a family of high achievers and raised by a single mother in poverty-stricken slums, yet you set your personal life goals while playing house." Yes, these details play a role in my adventures as I pursued personal plans and success--apart from God! Read on.

# CHAPTER TWO

# PLANNING MY LIFE

Fueled by my childhood experience, I continued the quest to rise above my humble beginnings. I vowed to work hard towards financial independence because I had witnessed the challenges and atrocities my Mom suffered at the hands of men. I also knew, from my mother's family history, that they had overcome worse challenges than what I faced. My uncles and aunts had prevailed over their circumstances, so I resolved that I would too. My biggest obstacle, though, was the fear of poverty. I sought academia and career advancement to bail me out. Nothing is wrong with being ambitious or seeking education, but these pursuits become problematic when God is left out.

The bulk of my young adult life was spent trying to figure out life. I relocated to the USA (America) when I was nineteen years old. From the time I left my family, who were still living in the slums, I knew there would be no turning back, so my only option was to stay the course. Granted, I had tough days; the earlier days of getting settled in America were frequently filled with tears. I would start crying but quickly fought back the tears while comforting myself, assuring myself to be strong. I recall coming home from my shift at work one night at about three a.m. in Newark, New Jersey. My feet hurt so badly that I took my shoes off and walked barefooted two miles to the room I rented for 75 dollars per week. I kept reassuring myself to stay strong as I walked through an extremely dangerous neighborhood.

Nevertheless, I knew that a new season would later dawn. I give credit to the Holy Spirit and glory to God for leading me through that season. The Holy Spirit guided me in such moments, step-by-step, about what to do next. The first six months in America were the most trying times, followed by other seasons of difficulties. The Holy Spirit remained a close counselor, teacher, and guide during those seasons until I started to ignore His directions and promptings. That was when I began the determined pursuit of My Plans.

At that point, I was already backslidden. I define the characteristics of backsliding in my terms, based on experience. The initial stages of the backsliding process are subtle and often characterized by seemingly reasonable or logical compromises. For example, I would say, "It's okay to work on Sundays to make extra money instead of attending church," or "It's okay to hang out with non-believers as long as I did not engage in what they were doing." There are a few common phrases: "Everyone is doing it," and "God understands," or "It is the trend." I did and said all that! However, slowly but surely, these ideas pulled me away from God. The next areas that were affected were my prayer and devotional life. Gradually, I noticed that I was no longer praying as fervently as before, and I struggled with reading the Bible. My heart eventually became hardened to God because my spirit, which should be nourished with prayer, devotion, and fellowship with others, was starved. It is quite possible to be a church-attending believer and live a backslidden life while attending church or serving in the church. This is because my hardened heart engaged in the formalities of church attendance and fellowship without total commitment, without surrender and intimacy with God. From my experience, I have concluded that a backslidden believer is someone who is neither intentionally committed to God or wholly surrendered to the Lordship of Jesus Christ, and the leadership of the Holy Spirit.

Frankly, a backslidden person cannot pinpoint exactly when the process began, because it often happens slowly; that was my case. I was actively involved in the church; however, I believe the slippery slope started after I finished college. I do not want to give excuses here, but I am not sure whether my transition to becoming a professional had anything to do with it, coupled with the pressure to support my family. I became a registered nurse at a young age; shortly after that, I was promoted to a management position. Maybe there is a tendency to reduce commitment to God when situations improve, as in my case, but God desires consistency in our commitment to Him in both good times and bad.

In addition to professional advancement, I realized that when I relocated for a new job, I did not have a good community of believers to connect with or a good church to attend for some time. Again, this is not an excuse to forsake independent prayer, Bible reading, fasting, or listening to the Holy Spirit. Believers are not supposed to stay in isolation but are meant to be connected to believers. My advice to young professionals would be to seek the Holy Spirit before you relocate, ask Him to help connect you with a group of believers who can hold you accountable and encourage you. Technology has also made it possible to connect with good churches and fellow believers through online platforms. Therefore, do your best to connect with fellow believers frequently. There is power in numbers; should someone fall, others can pick them up. Consider this advice from the wise King Solomon, *"Two are better than one because they have a good return for their labor: If either of them falls, one can help the other up. But pity anyone who falls and has no one to help them up. Also, if two lie down together, they will keep warm. But how can one keep warm alone? Though one may be overpowered, two can defend themselves. A cord of three strands is not quickly broken,"* Ecclesiastes 4:9-12 NIV.

For almost a decade, I was backslidden and managed my life the best I knew how. I honestly believe that God still had a measure of grace and mercy reserved for me during those years, even though I lived in utter rebellion against God. I can attest to this measure of God's grace, in this Psalm; *"what if the Lord had not been on our side? Let all Israel repeat: What if the Lord had not been on our side when people attacked us? They would have swallowed us alive in their burning anger. The waters would have engulfed us; a torrent would have overwhelmed us. Yes, the raging waters of their fury would have overwhelmed our very lives. Praise the Lord, who did not let their teeth tear us apart! We escaped like a bird from a hunter's trap. The trap is broken, and we are free! Our help is from the Lord, who made heaven and earth,"* Psalm 124:1-8 NKJV. I, too, was preserved by God, regardless of my resolution to plan my life without Him. Countless times, I experienced the Lord's blessings in most areas of my independent planning, while also experiencing disappointments and defeat in areas where I acted in total rebellion. Nevertheless, through both the blessings and the failures, God preserved my life from danger and death.

My ability to plan is an inherent gift that God gave me, and I am incredibly grateful for it. However, God was left out of my plans, goals, dreams, and ambitions. That amounts to self-worship or self-idolatry because my reliance was on human ability and power. There is a great deception in this because it breeds independence and self-reliance. The false belief that I could dictate terms and run my own life was deceptive and dangerous. Instead of enjoying success and blessings through the perfect will of God, I settled for second-best through the permissive will of God. God is His mercy and love, permitted what I wanted, although that was not necessarily the best for me. I deprived myself of the best God could offer when I left God entirely out of my affairs. God's will is good, acceptable, and perfect, see Romans 12:2 God through His perfect will directs our paths through what is suitable to accomplish the destiny He has for each of us.

Although I have briefly touched on the factors that led to my backsliding in this chapter, I would like to help you identify the signs of the pathway to backsliding for you to recognize and realign quickly to God. As shared, no one intentionally plans to backslide; the process starts subtly. Here are what to watch for

- Interruptions and inconsistencies in your prayer life and devotions that with time dwindle to not reading the Bible or praying at all

- Loss of hunger or passion for God. When the desire and fire for God or to serve God starts to fade away, or when there is loss of interest in your calling or service to God

- Focus efforts towards self-gratification, rather than God. More concerned in feeding the "flesh" what pleases the soul rather than your spirit

- Repeatedly disobeying the promptings and ignoring warnings of the Holy Spirit. Without honoring the Holy Spirit, one can become spiritually numb and spiritually blind and lose their sensitivity to the Holy Spirit and the Lord, making it difficult to hear God and respond accordingly to Him.

- Gifts of the Spirit and callings become less impactful than when one was committed to God.

- Tendencies to justify sin and rationalize sin and or compromise, providing reasons that are generally accepted by the standards of the world. These reasons or excuses contradict the word of God. Such reasons could be facts, but they are not true to the word of God. They often sound spiritual and are far from the truth. An example would be that like saying that white lies are not bad or sex outside marriage is not sinful because God understands

- Busy schedules that conflict with your weekly fellowship or church attendance. The conflicts in schedules will eventually lead to sporadic church attendance or no church attendance at all

- Attending church as a formality without a full commitment to God

- A change of heart where the heart focuses more on worldly things than God. Gradual accommodation, acceptance, and participation in worldly affairs; including opinions, fads, music, entertainment, past sinful patterns, and or materialism that is out of alignment with God

- Yielding to the company of unbelievers or ungodly friends you had disassociated with, befriending unbelievers, rekindling "old flames" with the hopes that you will convert them to Christ; however, the friends end up luring you away from God instead

- Distancing yourself from church, pastors, or fellow believers

- With time, one develops pride, arrogance, self -righteousness, and self-justification that further pulls the person away from God

# CHAPTER THREE

# THE ROOT OF SELF-RELIANCE

Self-reliance is [6]reliance on one's efforts and abilities. Synonyms for self-reliance include self-subsistence, independence, and self-sufficiency. Rick Thomas provides an excellent definition that applies to my testimony in his book *Boasting in Weakness: Overcoming Self-Reliance, 2017.* According to Thomas, self-sufficiency (self-reliance), [7] is "the self-deceiving, isolating process of trying to be stronger and stronger while resisting help from other people, and especially help from the LORD. It is the sinful desire to build a lifestyle and reputation that ends up discouraging someone from trusting God". Again, my situation fits all of the above.

Multiple factors contributed to my pursuit of independence. Whatever one's background may be, there are some common themes, or similarities of situations, that are relatable. I believe that life's experiences can shape how we think and act. In retrospect, I recognize that my background shaped my actions to a certain extent. I can see this now because I have come to understand and embrace my true identity in God. I recognize that I am established by what God says and what He has planned for me, so my past does not define me.

---

[6] www.merriam-webster.com/dictionary/self-reliance
[7] (Thomas, 2017) Thomas, Rick *Boasting in Weakness, Overcoming Self-Reliance* (2017)

There is nothing wrong with planning and setting goals. Personal success is not gained only through personal ambition or power but through partnership with God. In my case, while the fear of poverty and lack compelled me, other factors also contributed to my independence: fatherlessness, adversities, lack of security, fear of failure, strong ambition, and success. However, in hindsight, if I were, to summarize, everything that drove me to seek self-reliance, I would say it was unbelief. I did not believe that God would meet all my needs, and I did not consider I could be just as successful in Him. I related to God as the Creator, but not as a Father, which made me confront the issue of fatherlessness.

## Fatherlessness

I am the first-born of fraternal twins. Soon after we are born, my Mom brought me and my sister home from the hospital. My parents separated shortly after we were born. I last saw my father briefly when I was about three years old while staying with my grandmother.

A faulty belief system was the core of my plan to pursue success; I had the wrong idea about Who God is and what He intended to do. Though I knew God and had accepted Christ as my savior, I still saw God as a distant and impersonal Entity. I had read of Him as the omnipresent, omnipotent, loving Father, but the words had little relevance to me. Those attributes were just Christian lingo that I had heard repeatedly in my childhood. I also questioned God's love for me because I perceived Him as a judgmental Being. I believed that God was far away in heaven, and what happened to me was because He was judging me, or perhaps punishing me because I was backslidden. I did not believe God had all my best interests at heart, and I was not sure that He would fully support me in living a successful life. So, I took matters into my own hands.

Our perceptions of God often mirror our relationship with earthly fathers or father figures. It took me a long while to believe that God genuinely loved me. I often felt that He was angry with me for some unknown reason. I struggled to accept forgiveness from God, given the despicable things I had done when I was backslidden. I see how the devil used this wrong perception of God as an open door for developing even more harmful strongholds. Whereas I knew and believed in the power and works of God, I thought He favored others over myself. This belief drove me to seek affirmation in many areas, specifically, through career and personal advancement. Inherently, I am an overachiever!

I am glad to report that I have been delivered from the pain fatherlessness and continue to walk daily in this victory. I am emotionally, spiritually, physically, and psychologically healthy. The following are Scriptures of affirmation for the fatherless: The Almighty God is my Father," *Sing to God, sing praises to His name, extol Him who rides on the clouds, by His name Yah, and rejoice before Him. A father of the fatherless, a defender of widows, is God in His holy habitation. God sets the solitary in families; He brings out those bound into prosperity. Psalm 68:4-6b NKJV.* The Passion Translation says, *"To the fatherless, He is a father. To the widow, he is a champion friend. To the lonely, he makes them part of a family. To the prisoners, he leads into prosperity until they sing for joy. This is our Holy God in his Holy Place!" Psalm 68:5-6a, TPT.* If you only have one parent or have lost both parents, consider making God your "All in All". Submit to the Lordship of Jesus and embrace God's assurance of love, guidance, provision, and protection. I encourage you to declare in the following Scriptures over yourself daily and memorize them:

- *The Lord watches over foreigners, He upholds the widow and the fatherless, but the way of the wicked he brings to ruin," Psalm 146:9, ESV.*

- *But you, God, see the trouble of the afflicted; you consider their grief and take it in hand. The victims commit themselves to You; You are the helper of the fatherless". Psalm 10:14, NIV.*

- *Defending the fatherless and the oppressed, so that mere earthly mortals will never again strike terror, Psalm 10:18, NIV.*

- *Because I rescued the poor, who cried for help, and the fatherless who had none to assist them, Job 29:12, NIV.*

## Strict Upbringing

I was raised by a community of relatives, mostly from the maternal side of the family. My childhood was with grandparents until I turned seven years old and resumed living with my Mom in Nakuru, Kenya. Mom was strict and had high expectations for all of us. There was no time for small-talk or love-talk; most conversations centered around academics and household chores. There were no words of affirmation or love from Mom; this is common practice in the African culture. We once joked with friends that when you grew up African, you just knew your parents loved you; they did not have to say it.

Mom often expressed strictness through criticism, which often left me feeling that whatever I did was not good enough. I often received a whooping if I did not place first in academics. She strongly instilled the responsibility of the first-born, telling me that I was accountable for the rise and fall of my siblings, and the family in general. In most African cultures, the first-born child, often bears a high level of responsibility. Such upbringing is, therefore, not uncommon. My aunts and uncles had equally high expectations of us. Indeed, there were no written rules about being and doing the best, but we all knew that they expected great things of us. Our family was tightly-knit; permitting any adult relative to discipline anyone else's child. In most African cultures, the proverb is: "It takes a village to raise a child!" Looking back, though, I believe Mom was just doing her best to care for all five of us. She served as both father and mother, and for a single mom earning minimum wage, that was tough. I applaud her sacrifice and commitment to us and appreciate Mom's dedication to us. She never gave up, despite the cultural connotation of single motherhood in the African culture.

I hesitate to ascribe my perfectionistic nature solely to the influence of my strict upbringing because, I liked order and structure from a young age. I now realize that I have the gift of excellence and organization; however, without God, that translates to perfectionism. In in my case perfectionism was characterized by such extreme neatness and organization that I would be upset if a comb were placed in the wrong direction. It is highly likely that perfectionism translated to Obsessive-Compulsive Disorder (OCD). The other effect of this strict upbringing was a strong ambition to succeed. This was not wrong because I enjoyed the self-gratification of achieving my goals, whether they were academic or career-inspired. But my challenge came when I felt like I just needed to keep on accomplishing more; consequently, I pushed myself hard. I had high expectations that I would crash down in a strong sense of failure if I did not achieve them. My ambition was also driven by the dire need to rescue my family from the slums. I was determined to work hard for myself and my family.

## Responsible Child Expectations

I have observed that most families have a child that is responsible. This child is often looked up to and sought to make decisions in the family. That person is often the go-to person, irrespective of birth order. This behavior is called destructive parentification. [8]In parentification, children take caregiving responsibilities and assume such a role for their parents, siblings, or other family members, at the expense of their own

---

[8]  https://www.youniversetherapy.com/post/the-trauma-of-parentification

developmental needs. In my case, I just happened to be the first-born.

I started functioning at this level of responsibility when I was seven years old. Most of it started when Mom delegated house chores that had to be completed on time. I had to watch over my siblings. I was seven years old when I first learned how to cook. As I grew older, my job description expanded to "other duties as necessary." By age ten, Mom left me to manage the house and my siblings while she was away. I grow up very quickly as a result of this. I believed my siblings depended on my support in their upbringing, so I often acted with my family in mind. This expectation caused me to push myself, often denying myself for the sake of the family.

I believe that every person has a level of responsibility for our families and siblings, but not to extremes. God is responsible for every one of His creations. When someone takes on the responsibility to meet the needs of someone's life, that idea can become a form of idolatry. Fellow humans are not in charge of another individual's plans; God is. Adults should not expect a child to carry the responsibility of managing a family; that weight is too much for one so young. I believe in setting boundaries and sharing responsibility, especially later when adults and can fend for themselves. I also believe in helping someone who takes the initiative to improve their quality of life; such people are worth supporting. Although such expectations are real, wisdom and discernment are needed so that caregivers do not end up in unhealthy patterns, unnecessarily depleting their resources for the sake of others. Through experience, I learned that helping others can quickly turn into expectations; the person getting help starts demanding more. This situation is not only abusive but exploitative. Balancing responsibilities and setting reasonable boundaries are vital to maintain enough resources to live well and help someone else when the Lord directs.

# Disguised Sarcasm

Our family endured mockery and discrimination at different levels, but the most challenging time was when the insults and ridicule came from within our circle. There are specific comments that I have hoped would cease over time, but I have continue to hear them. Most of what was said and done to us arose from to our socio-economic status and because we were fatherless. Unless God changes someone's heart, no matter how much we accomplished, I have learned that the denigrating comments towards me will never change. I realize that no one has control over what anyone else thinks about them. I am determined to remain unoffendable and still relate those relatives and friends through Christ's Love.

Everyone wants to be acknowledged, respected, and accepted among friends or family. I mostly suppressed my emotions, but the most painful occurrences were when my siblings told me what had been done or said to them by relatives. As the big sister, I purposely shielded them from such disparagement. We occasionally cried together secretly, but I am also aware of private tears shed by my Mom and siblings independently. Such behaviors stirred my ambition to improve our quality of life and change our family name, but I did not realize that only God can do that. God is impartial.... *"God chose things the world considers foolish to shame those who think they are wise. And he chose things that are powerless to shame those who are powerful,"* 1 Corinthians 1:27, NLT.

There is a promise, *"God sets high the lowly and those who mourn He brings to safety,"* Job 5:11, KJV. This promise is for anyone who may have been ostracized, mocked, or humiliated in their upbringing. Encouraging someone to let go is easier said than done. But if you have had similar experiences, I encourage you to forgive, bless, and love your perpetrators. Ask the Holy Spirit to help you deal with offenses quickly. Do not allow what people say to lodge in your heart, because, if left unresolved, such words and comments can result in strongholds, false beliefs, and unhealthy attitudes that can negatively influence your life. Below is a prayer for breaking negative words:

*Father in the Name of Jesus Christ, I thank You for loving me unconditionally. I thank You for inscribing on the days of my life in Your book. I bless Your Name because what you have said about me remains unchallenged. Lord I ask that forgive me for any negative word or curse I have spoken over anyone. I repent of engaging in false conversations about others through, gossip, slander, and rumors. I repent of opinions, judgements, and criticisms I may have passed on others. Forgive me Lord. Now Lord, I forgive everyone (state the name of the person) who has spoken negatively over me. I forgive them and let them go. Through the Blood of Jesus and in the Name of Jesus, I break the power of every negative word, name, spell, curse, evil prayer, chant, and false prophesy that has been spoken over me. I renounce negative identities and false perceptions of what they made me feel. I break every stronghold in my mind that is tied to those negative names, evil wishes, words, evil prayers, false prophesies, and curses. I command afflicting spirits associated with those names to leave my life right now in the Name of Jesus. I free myself from their bonds and yokes. In the Name of Jesus, I now declare my freedom. I walk in the true identity that you have predestined for me as Your son or daughter. In the Name of Jesus. Amen.*

## False Personal Expectations

I developed false expectations of myself. Fear of failure provoked me to drive myself and be overly ambitious., I kept pushing myself higher, while I also beat and condemned myself at every little setback. But God did not intend for believers to have such a lifestyle. We are to live a life of hope, peace, joy, and faith. Through faith in God and a good understanding of who we are in Christ, we can base our lives on the promises and plans God has for us, as we walk in the blessings of His will here on earth, as it is in heaven. God's ideas of success are different from ours, but they always lead to peace and fruitfulness in the end.

# Poverty

In a recent conversation with my brother, we reflected on the earlier part our lives and wondered what we could have done differently, based on our current knowledge. One topic was our inability to account for wasted years that we could have used to attain our doctoral degrees. My brother and I are seven years apart in age, so I could not help but laugh at how driven we are. As we spoke, I disclosed how determined I was to attain advanced college degrees and climb the career ladder. My brother responded that he often felt like he needed to be doing more and more. I quickly recognized how similar we are in our highly-driven quest for success in life. While pondering the discussion, I realized that we are both still running from the extreme poverty of our beginnings! We had nothing to fall back on in Kenya. Relocating to the USA was the ticket to a new life, in our case, a new promised land. All my siblings have an inherent determination to excel in life and overcome our past; however, it seems that this overdriven ambition rested more intensely on my brother and me. The race to escape poverty quickly fueled the self-reliance. But acquiring more money and having great careers does not necessarily equal success. The positions God makes available have a lasting legacy. When our ambitions and dreams are God-driven, we can enjoy the blessings and be fruitful and prosperous. This focus on God is my definition of success.

# Life's Adversities

Hardship can either make you or break you. When I faced a barrage of cyclical adversities, I took matters into my own hands. Some difficulties were a result of my poor choices. God allowed other predicaments to happen to mature me. Other setbacks were opposition from satan, the enemy of destinies. If I could have discovered the source of the troubles, that would have helped make them easier to overcome, learn from, or avoid. But I could not discern spiritual matters in my backslidden state, so I resorted to trying to fix the situations the best way I knew how. Some mishaps left me so exhausted and depressed that when I recovered from them, I swore never to allow a repeat of the experience. Eventually, I resolved to build emotional walls to protect myself, but as a result, I became guarded and rigid. This was my defense system that evolved in making harmful vows such as, "I will never do this again," "I will never let someone do this," "Nobody will ever... "the list of the "nevers" goes on.

Negative vows are binding; they grant satan legal rights to activate and reinforce the vow you made. The reinforced vows then perpetuate attacks from the enemy. This root is one of the origins of negative cycles. Breaking soul ties and covenants from such vows can stop the cycles of adversity. Excluding God from misfortunes can compound the adversity, but there is encouragement even in that place. God delights in His dear children when they submit everything to Him and seek His help in time of need. Scriptures say He is a Friend who is closer than a brother, see (Proverbs 18:24, NIV).

## Betrayal, Rejection, and Abandonment

Despite having a large supportive extended family, my immediate family of six grew up in the protection and shelter of our God right there in the slums. Our last residence in the slums was in Nyalenda in Kisumu, Kenya. Mom ensured that we became actively involved in church and in devotion to God from the day we were born again. Family Bible devotion and prayer time were a must. So, by God's grace all of us were well-versed in Scripture, prayer, and knowledge of the works of the Holy Spirit. Each of us knew the voice of the Holy Spirit. But we were naïve, trusting that anyone who said they were born-again would be honest and dependable. We believed this as children, but we were shocked by our experiences as adults. Whenever a Christian betrayed, extorted, rejected, or disappointed us, we reacted with utter surprise; we just could not comprehend that Christians would do such hideous things. In another recent conversation with my brother, he shared the same sentiment, saying, "'Polly, what people repeatedly do to you can make you become what you do not want to be!"

What people put us through can, indeed, change us. As committed believers, we can respond by exercising the fruit of the Spirit, love, self-control, and still see people through the eyes of Christ. However, without Christ, such experiences cause us to distance ourselves from people and resort to "just doing my own thing," or result in a perception that, "I don't need anybody." Such conclusions appear convincing at the moment, but as time goes on, if not renounced, they can also lead to isolation and discouragement. We are more susceptible to the enemy's attacks when we are alone. We need one another; the best course of action is to forgive and ask God to bring genuine friendships that align with the destiny He has for you.

## Negativity

Negativity is experienced through personal perception, environmentally, or by spoken words. These all have the potential to impact behavior, attitudes, and personality. Living in the slums was not the best environment, so we were all incredibly grateful to God for His divine protection and countless interventions on our behalf. But the slum environment was a catalyst that boosted our determination to do whatever it took to escape that atmosphere. Although this did not impact me, a negative self-perception can lead to overindulgence to try to overcome the negativity. When someone frequently encounters negativity, there is a tendency to overcompensate, Anyone subjected to belittlement may resort to unhealthy behavior to numb the pain, But that path can lead to life-threatening addictions or isolation. Perception does not equal truth; neither is it a fact. It is a subjective experience. What is perceived is not necessarily the truth.

Our family was significantly impacted by the negative words spoken over us, often from close friends and relatives. As the oldest, I frequently observed people as they ridiculed my Mom; and over time, that transferred to my siblings and me; we were also mocked and called names within the same circle of friends and relatives. Comments like these were frequently spoken: "What will you ever amount to?" or, "you will be just like your mom," or "you will stay in poverty or work as housemaids." The constant vituperation caused me to distance myself, and of course, also escalated the drive to escape from it and improve my situation. Sadly, such negativity led me to make more internal vows and, to a certain extent, increased the personal pressure to change the "perception."

## Impatience

A long-standing history of delayed answers to prayer urged me to take matters into my own hands. This delay mirrors the point I made earlier, regarding unbelief and doubt. When answers to my petitions did not come fast enough, I began to doubt that God would show up at all, so I resorted to seeking answers my way. However, I have since learned that independently fixing a problem can produce an outcome, but the result often involves much toil. God, on the other side, can provide just a simple idea, coupled with His favor, to bring results with minimal effort. I have learned that a better plan is to wait on God instead of seeking my alternatives.

My desperation and impatience led me to abusive and unhealthy relationships. I ended up attracting fair-weather friends and people of questionable character. I did not even have enough in common with some people to sustain a relationship. Often those associations took more from me than I received. Some people were leeches and predators. Watch out for them! Serious discernment is required here. I believe in balanced give-and-take friendships and relationships, where both parties encourage and support each other. Those unhealthy relationships were doomed from the beginning and set me up to be vulnerable to emotional, physical, financial, spiritual exploitation or abuse. In a bid for acceptance, I became too accommodating to such false friends, and they took more than they gave. Please take a lesson from me: Whenever you are in the company of people who seek your help, but then you see them advancing with what you gave them while you remain stagnant, know that you are being robbed! Be leery of such one-sided friendships. You could be wasting your time, skills, and resources. You could lose your money, your reputation, or your influence, not to mention your self-respect. Be cautious of people who do not reciprocate your overtures of friendship.

Impatience can cause people to resort to manipulation to obtain the results they want. Some employees sabotage their co-workers for recognition or promotion. Dating couples manipulate one another for what they want. People get married in haste, sometimes for the wrong reasons. Others falsify records to obtain higher incentives. Manipulation is a form of witchcraft because it is control or coercion. Witchcraft is an abominable sin that God hates. Anyone practicing witchcraft is lazy and weak! I believe in being diligent in earning rewards from the work of your own hands.

In the journey with God, He sometimes provides things instantly, and other things He will release at the right time, often much later. Scripture tells us to wait on God in persevering faith, trusting that God will answer us at the right time. God's promises are yes and Amen. God is also sure to perform His Word, just as He promised. He is the God who hears our prayers and answers them, trust waits upon the Lord. *"Wait for the LORD; be strong and let your heart take courage; wait for the Lord!"* *Psalm 27:14, ESV.*

## Need for Independence

There is something good about being independent and self-sufficient. A sign of maturity is when we can take care of our households and life without depending on others, which brings a sense of accomplishment and responsibility that has been well-fulfilled. The quest for independence began early in my childhood when I played house and strategized my life. As I grew up, I strove for this independence through various forms, through careers, relationships, and decision-making. Occasionally, I was lured to compare myself to others who seemed to be living a great life. I had to make a better life for myself. I had no choice, though; when I started living by myself at nineteen years old after relocating to the USA, I had to make most of my decisions because my Mom was still far away in Africa. I made some bad choices at times, but I also thank the Holy Spirit for guiding me in my young-adult life. Gaining independence is an outstanding achievement. Now, that I am a mentor, my main goal for a mentee is to help them acquire the skills they need to function independently and mentor others in return, but I have to teach them how to succeed in God's way.

## Need for Security

My childhood experiences heightened my need for security. I cannot say that I had any safe person to fall back to when the going got rough. Poverty played a role in pushing me to attain a sense of security, whether I accomplished it through education or career advancement. I recall making negative vows. One of them was a vow to be financially secure and never have to depend on anyone. I also felt compelled to work long hours without rest, at times, to attain that security. Though these were great goals, they still reflect my self -reliance rather than trust God for provision. To say, "never depend on anyone, also meant never to depend on God. You can see how such a vow is damaging and underscores the power of God to meet all needs!

Finally, the root of my self-reliance was a deep desire for affirmation. Lacking affirmation from my parents, I sought it through professional achievements and perfectionism. I was an executive reporting to the board of directors and the president of a company at thirty-six years old. I thought that my attainments would attract better opportunities and relationships. This idea ended up being a double-edged sword. I attained great career opportunities, but was unable to maintain healthy friendships and relationships, as I seemed to be a threat to the very people I wished to befriend. Most friends ended up exploiting me instead. Others sought friendship with me for what they could acquire, and then there were others whose agenda was powered by envy and unhealthy competition. On one occasion, while assisting someone, the person told me blatantly that they wanted to be better than me, so they chose the career I took, bought four different cars in three years, and relocated twice to make that happen. This person was someone I had supported with tooth, nail, and sweat! I quickly ended that friendship.

Since my life was bereft of affirmation, I realized that I did things to affirm myself. Most of this came through setting high personal standards and being overly principled, conscientious, organized, and regimented. I have renounced and continued to shun these extreme tendencies since they often caused additional stress and brought a sense of failure whenever I did not meet my expectations. Stress can be self-inflicted. I have since stopped being so hard on myself! Praise God for His saving grace!

I am still working to overcome the need for affirmation. Lately, I realized that I would delay making decisions because I needed someone to validate them. I believe the issues of fatherlessness, uncertainty about God's care, and fear of failure are contributors to this. I have since renounced these and I am committed to trusting the Holy Spirit for guidance. While having my "moments with God" (moments with God are reflections that

I engage with God in dialogue), in 2018, God admonished to "trust the Holy Spirit." When believers collaborate with the Holy Spirit, tune in to Him, remain sensitive to Him, trust Him, and obey, they are assured of making wise, productive decisions. So, I encourage you to rely on the Holy Spirit, trust His voice and guidance, and follow His directions. The best affirmations and validations are from God through the Holy Spirit. Such validations never fail to bolster confidence.

Moreover, each Spirit-filled born-again believer already receives affirmation since Jesus Christ them. When people receive Christ, the Holy Spirit guarantees that they are children of God. This new identity validates them.

Affirmation has positive implications too. The need for affirmation is godly. Believers can affirm themselves by citing the Word of God based on the identity He has given. Examples of affirmations are, God loves and accepts them, they are co-heirs with Christ, are victorious in Christ, they have the mind of Christ; Christians we hear God clearly because the Lord is the Shepherd and His sheep know His voice; each person is fearfully and wonderfully created, God's children have everything that pertains to life and godliness! There are many more affirmations in Scripture for each believer!

Our needs can also be met through others. Although all believers together are of one body, each one has something unique to offer for the success of the Body of Christ. My choice to be solely independent deprived me of this great wealth of expertise, blessing, and wisdom that others had. I believe that God created people to live in a community to help meet each other's needs. We can also encounter God through others. God wants us to experience such fellowship and support with Him and through others. We can get some of our needs met in the community, but God is ultimately the Giver of everything we need.

# CHAPTER FOUR

# CONSEQUENCES OF
# THE INDEPENDENT LIFESTYLE

The self-sufficient attitude led me to rationalize and justify my actions because I had little sense of community or accountability. Howbeit, such attitudes arose because I had been repeatedly disappointed by people I relied on for direction or advice. However, I know that God is always available whenever I need His counsel, *"God is our refuge and strength, a very present help in trouble,"* Psalm 46:1, ESV. God provides counsel when we ask Him *"if any of you lacks wisdom, let him ask God, who gives generously to all without reproach, and it will be given him. But let him ask in faith, with no doubting, for the one who doubts is like a wave of the sea that is driven and tossed by the wind,"* James 1:5-6, ESV. Another promise says, *"call to Me (God), and I will answer you and will tell you great and hidden things that you have not known",* Jeremiah 33:3, ESV.

An independent mindset had me convinced that I had to fend for myself. Such thinking also produces negative vows that I often heard among the ladies: "I don't need anyone's help," "I don't need a man" or, "I am good by myself." Unless we renounce them, such comments are binding because they are doorways to isolation, loneliness, and depression. As we age, we tend to value the need for fellowship and community, having people that we can count on around for assistance. I did things with ease when I was nineteen that I dread doing now, like climbing up to change a light bulb. I would rather have my nephews do that. We need each other.

There are conditions to God's blessings and success in life. When I lived contrary to God's commands and depended solely on my efforts, I was bound to reap the fruit of those endeavors. I first heard the following quote from Dr. Charles Stanley, who teaches that *"we reap what we sow, more than we sow, and later than we sow."* What we do, whether good or evil, has an outcome, and the harvest is often greater than the initial sowing! Here is another comprehensive principle on the same subject by Dr. Joseph Peck of Empower 2000;*"you reap what you sow, you reap more than you sow, you reap later than you sow, you reap where you sow, the soil you sow in determines the amount or volume of harvest you will reap".* Romans 1:28 is a great scripture to help us understand what happens when people ignore God. I first heard of this scripture when I was fourteen years old, through a traveling evangelist who was conducting house fellowships in Kisumu, Kenya. The evangelist taught on the signs of a reprobate mind. God leaves us to follow our own path sometimes. Failure to heed His instructions leads to a reprobate mind. The verse reads: *"and even as they did not like to retain God in their knowledge, God gave them over to a reprobate mind, to do those things which are not convenient, Romans 1:28.* The TPT translation of the same verses says, *"and because they thought it was worthless to embrace the true knowledge of God, God gave them over to a worthless mindset, to* break all rules of proper conduct". The ESV translation says, and since they did not see fit to acknowledge God, God gave them up to a debased mind to do what ought not to be done.

When anyone walks in constant rebellion and neglects God's standards, God will leave them to their free will. In Genesis 6:3, God warns that He will not strive with man forever. The following are other outcomes of my independent lifestyle:

# Carnality

Carnality is a mindset or lifestyle that is of void the guidance of the Holy Spirit and the Word of God. Carnality ignores God. In my case, carnality operated through my intellect. I was very philosophical and analytical. My first step, when presented with a problem, would be to evaluate the various options for the solution. That sounds sensible, right? But I approached the problem from a human standpoint instead of beginning with the most critical step: consulting God. Of course, you can imagine how that worked out: I would list all the solutions and try them one by one until each solution failed. Some of the failures were exhausting and costly, and then I would finally decide to ask God what He had to say. If I had sought God first, I would have received a word or a direction that would have brought the breakthrough sooner. Jesus taught us to seek first the Kingdom of God, and everything else shall be added to us; (Matthew 6:33 and Colossians 3: 1-4 NIV). Seeking God involves inquiring from Him first, waiting for an answer, and then only doing what He directs us to do.

Two kings in the Old Testament, David, and Hezekiah; provide excellent examples of how to handle problems. Scriptures mention how they asked God for direction. David's account of seeking the Lord says, *"now there was a famine in the days of David for three years, year after year. And David sought the face of the Lord"*, 2 Samuel 21:1, ESV. King David had a history of seeking the Lord in most things, especially issues related to war. There are multiple accounts of David making inquiries of the Lord concerning key battle strategies; (at least six times), in the books of 1 and 2 Samuel. Whenever David sought the Lord, God responded with a solution. The other example that encourages me often is King Hezekiah. He sought the Lord in two critical moments. When his enemies threatened to invade his kingdom; (see 2 Kings 19), his first response to the ominous report was to seek the Lord through prayer. The second incident was when Hezekiah fell ill (Isaiah 38:2), and he prayed again. King Hezekiah opted to seek God first. God honored King Hezekiah's humility in both incidents, first by destroying his enemies, then by healing him.

In contrast to the favorable outcomes of kings David and Hezekiah, King Asa suffered a dire consequence that he might have avoided, because he did not seek the Lord nor trust Him. The Bible concludes the history of King Asa with, "and in the thirty and ninth year of his reign Asa was diseased in his feet; his disease was exceeding great: *yet in his disease, he sought not the LORD, but the physicians. So, Asa rested with his fathers; he died in the forty-first year of his reign*", 2 Chronicles 16:12-13, ESV. King Asa is an example of someone who relied on the expertise of men but not God. Granted physicians were likely knowledgeable but Christ is our wisdom; He can diagnose and heal any condition. We should seek God first before entreating humans. God warns against trusting in human intelligence- Psalm 146:3 NIV. "Do not put your trust in princes, in human beings, who cannot save. God prefers that we commit our ways to the Lord, and He shall establish them." Proverbs 3:6, NIV. When God establishes our ways, He does exceedingly more than what we ask or think, when we ask according to His will (Ephesians 3:20 and 1 John 5:14). Let us partner with the Holy Spirit in all things.

## Comparison and Insecurity

I have added these topics here just from observations in life. From an early age, I purposed not to compare myself with others or boast. I am a confident person who believes that healthy competition builds strength. By contrast, bitter contention provokes striving and putting others down to win. Such behaviors are a result of insecurity. All that striving and negativity depletes one's resources and leads to destruction, especially if one is striving to be like another by following the standards of this world. The most stressful path anyone can pursue is to acquire something just because another person has done so for the sake of appearances or status symbols. They call this, "Keeping up with the Jones's. This constant striving results in covetousness, anxiety, and dissatisfaction.

Unhealthy competition and comparison produce selfishness, self-promotion, and narcissistic tendencies; For the person involved, life becomes all about them. Then relationships can become a stepping-stone to get all they can from people, instead of what they can offer to others. Co-workers can engage in office politics while they jockey for position and favor with the boss. Some people take advantage of hardworking people; by exploiting the generosity of others, some go to the extent of destroying marriages, all in a quest for self-gratification and significance. But God has specific goals for each person who commits their life to Him. God has individualized paths that lead to each person's destiny. But by competing and comparing ourselves with others, we forfeit valuable steps towards our unique calling in a futile attempt to walk in someone else's future. That is like trying to force your feet into someone else's shoes that are either too big or too small; severely hampering your journey is such ill-fated shoes.

Insecurity can trigger suppressed trauma through a faulty understanding of our identity in Christ. This self-doubt undermines the potential of our God-given abilities. When we submit to God, the Spirit of God will guide us in wisdom, knowledge, and understanding of how to use our skills effectively to prosper. Bezalel is a great example of a man whom God filled with His Spirit to design and create components and accessories for God's temple. See *Exodus 31: 1-6 ESV: "the Lord said to Moses, "see, I have called Bezalel ......... I have filled him with the Spirit of God, ability, and intelligence, with knowledge and all craftsmanship, to devise artistic designs, to work in gold, silver, and bronze, in cutting stones for setting, and in carving wood, to work in every craft. And behold, I have appointed with him Oholiab, ....... And I have given to all able men ability, that they may make all that I have commanded you".* You too can trust that God has anointed you to be effective and progressive through your skills; you will prosper!

Challenges that seem overwhelming may trigger insecurity, which sparks a crippling sense of incompetence, dysfunction, traumatic experiences, and a false perception of our identity. God wants to deliver people and set them free. God can heal emotional hurts, too; seek ministry with your church or through Christian counselors if you need emotional healing. Also, remember that God knows our inadequacies, and He is not limited by them. God already factored our strengths and weakness in the plans He made for us. Despite our flaws, we can be confident that God will enable us to accomplish His purposes in our lives. Moses was insecure, but God empowered Him to confront a nation. Gideon was a farmer, and yet, God used Him to lead an army. David was a shepherd, but he became the most revered king, whose kingdom God has established forever (2 Samuel 7:12-13).

## Self-Reliance

Self-reliance and independence are similar in that they both stem from dependence on one's strength, skills, and achievements. Problem-solving and organization are inherent gifts that I have. Left responsible for the household as a child, decision making was critical especially when my Mom was away. As an adult, my educational and career achievements also allowed me to work in leadership positions that often-required troubleshooting and thinking on my toes. This combination made a great recipe to rationalize and justify my actions to such a point that I automatically resorted to problem-solving without asking God. I had answers at my fingertips, but they did not originate through seeking God. I tend to look for logic and reason in everything, and as long as those were present, I felt that whatever decision I made was legitimate.

None of the statements in the above paragraph are wrong, exactly, except that I came to learn that despite one's abilities, knowing the right time for executing something is crucial. The means of execution is also critical to prevent failure or a missed opportunity. If a company tries a winter product in the summer, the sales will not meet the full potential because the timing is wrong. Presenting ideas and goals at the right time is paramount. Counsel at the wrong time is just noise, which will not be readily embraced. Only God, through the Holy Spirit, can show us how to be effective in these areas. Submitting all ideas and seeking God's guidance for each situation is crucial because although situations may be similar, the strategies for success may be different.

Never assume and implement an old strategy for a new challenge. The Holy Spirit may have a different approach to the issue. Jesus Christ demonstrated this so well; He healed the blind: one by telling him to wash his eyes, the other, touching the eyes, and another, by mixing soil and applying to the eyes. All the blind men received their sight, but the strategies for healing were different. (see Matthew 9: 27-30; John 9:6 and Luke 18:35-43, NKJV).

King David's reliance on God for guidance in warfare is another excellent example of the timing and application of different strategies to win. Every time King David inquired of the Lord; the Lord responded with a different strategy. Look at this example; ..."*and the Philistines came up yet again and spread out in the Valley of Rephaim. And when David inquired of the Lord, he said, You shall not go up; go around to their rear and come against them opposite the balsam trees. And when you hear the sound of marching in the tops of the balsam trees, then rouse yourself, for then the Lord has gone out before you to strike down the army of the Philistines. And David did as the Lord commanded him and struck down the Philistines from Geba to Gezer,*" 2 Samuel 5:22-25, ESV. God has different strategies for each issue. Even parents can attest that they do not interact with every child in the same way, because children respond in different ways, depending on their situation. When seeking God becomes our priority, He will provide a strategy for solving each problem.

Finally, the instigator of self-reliance is pride that springs from a need to be in control. Such ignorance and arrogance led me to think that I could dictate and control God, by submitting my needs to Him with petitions of exactly how I wanted them to manifest. I would first make independent decisions, then ask God to bless them and bring them to pass. Let us be like King David, who had a habit of asking God for direction.

Our Lord Jesus and King David are great examples to reflect on in this section because both were anointed and skilled in their callings, yet they humbled themselves to seek God. I am often touched by the fact that Jesus only did what He saw His Father do in His ministry on earth. He was the Godhead, yet He did not consider Himself equal to God; instead, He humbled Himself, sought God, obeyed, and only did what He saw God the Father do, to the end of His ministry. Resist pride and any temptation to rely on your strengths or accolades. Instead, *"trust in the Lord with all your heart and lean not on your understanding; in all your ways acknowledge Him, and He shall direct your path,"* Proverbs 3:5-6, NKJV. Commit to reading the Bible daily as well; allow God to guide you through His Word. God's Word is wisdom. God's Word is a lamp unto our feet and a light to our paths: (Psalm 119:105, NKJV). Let God's light, which is His Word, guide you. Jesus Christ is the Word as well. He is the brightest guiding Light!

## Indecision, Doublemindedness, and Loss of Focus

A mind that is guided by God is peaceful and focused. But a mind that is not guided by God is susceptible to confusion, disorientation, and indecision. Such was my mind when I relied on myself. Knowing what I know now, I now realize, that my independence created potential entry points that the enemy used to oppress my mind.

Inherently, I am focused, I plan and strategize in advance; I have been doing it since I was ten years old. But when I was backslidden, there was a five-year period when I could not set goals or stick to them. I noticed that I lost focus while I was in a relationship with a man, I thought I would marry. I severely struggled with decision making and in my career during that season as well. Twice I enrolled in and paid for courses that I never finished. I even graduated with a third master's degree, which was below what I had planned. I have continued to use what I studied from that degree, but it was not the preferred degree. In confusion, I attempted to open three businesses, but they never took off. I believe I was striving to fill a void by doing all these things, a void that could not be filled even by being in a relationship. My actions were indecisive. The solution would have been simply to ask God for direction! Then I would not have wasted time and money, pursuing unproductive businesses, or engaging in unhealthy relationships.

Satan often fights our destiny and identity. Confusion, indecision, and a clouded mind are some of the ways he tries to divert one's focus and destiny. The ability to use sound judgment in decision-making was a challenge when I was confused. On the contrary, God provides order and peace. God assures us of a peaceful mind in this promise; "*You (God) keep him in perfect peace, whose mind is stayed on you because he trusts in You.*" Isaiah 26:3, NIV. God is orderly in all He does, but whenever there is confusion or cycles of erroneous outcomes, these are signs of mental attacks from the enemy. These attacks should be dealt with by renewing the mind with the word of God, through prayer and obedience to God's voice. "God *is not the author of confusion but peace*", 1 Corinthians 14:33a, ESV.

Moreover, when we cast all our cares, anxieties, and worries to God, He promises to give us peace that surpasses human understanding. That peace is Jesus Christ himself, *"for He Himself is our peace, who has made both one, and has broken down the middle wall of separation, having abolished in His flesh the enmity, that is, the law of commandments contained in ordinances, to create in Himself one new man from the two, thus making peace, and that He might reconcile them both to God in one body through the cross, thereby putting to death the enmity. And He came and preached peace to you who were afar off and to those who were near. For through Him, we both have access by one Spirit to the Father.", Ephesians 2:14-18, NKJV.* God encourages us to, "be anxious for nothing, but in everything by prayer and supplication, with thanksgiving, let your requests be made known to God; and the peace of God, which surpasses all understanding, will guard your hearts and minds through Christ Jesus," Philippians 4:6-7, NKJV.

Double-mindedness is the most frustrating problem because it leads to cycles of incomplete tasks and procrastination. Double-mindedness is equivalent to having two hearts: two minds with opposing views at different times. A double-minded person is inconsistent and vacillates from day to day. There are two adverse effects of double-mindedness. First is indecision: reasoning from either with God's Word as the or using the world's standards basis of our decisions. Secondly, division: the double-minded person is unaware that their very soul is divided and works against their destiny, *"a double-minded man is unstable in all his ways," James 1:8, NKJV.*

Past trauma can cause double-mindedness. Examples are trauma from molestation, abandonment, rejection, divorce, betrayal, illness, accidents, or abusive relationship. Loss of a job, a loved one, or even the pain of betrayal, can cause friction in the mind that results in spiritual, mental, and emotional instability. My history was littered by these traumas. A double-minded person is never "settled" in their purpose, and ultimately, they cannot adequately fulfill God's plans for their lives. This issue is more than a deliverance issue. The double-minded person needs to be healed from the damage they have suffered. The soul became divided due to the inability to handle the trauma, primarily if it occurred at a young age. Trauma separates the mind into compartments so the person sometimes cannot maintain their sanity. The ungodly or false personality that has been given influence over their thinking must be destroyed. The person can experience real stability and the lasting change of single-mindedness to think and focus clearly.

Whenever you find yourself unable to concentrate, make concrete decisions, or focus, you should renounce, rebuke, and command the demonic spirits of confusion, doublemindedness, vagabond, and wandering spirits to leave in the Name of Jesus. Ask God to restore a sound mind and clarity to you. Declare that you have the mind of Christ to influence you according to 1 Corinthians 2:16. Declare over yourself: *"God has not given me a spirit of fear but of power and love and a sound mind"*, 2 Timothy 1:7, NKJV.

Listed below are signs of double-mindedness that I recently researched. There is a demonic spirit of double-mindedness that is often coupled with a spirit of confusion, passivity, and procrastination. In my backslidden state, I did not know that I had a stronghold of double-mindedness. But I know God delivered me of this too when He delivered me from depression and suicidal thoughts. However, I have studied the subject and identified the following symptoms. Although I did not exhibit all signs, these are indicative of demonic strongholds that should be broken. If you recognize any of these symptoms, break them in the Mighty Name of Jesus.

- Repetitive cycles of starting a project or goal without completing them. Fear, confusion, anxiety, or distractions can cause this break in clarity and focus

- Inability to seek new opportunities or take reasonable risks due to fear of failure or fear of making unwise decisions

- Indecision may manifest through knowing the right decision but not having the resolve to decide or teetering between decisions. Such a person is always wavering in the middle, always second-guessing themselves

- Racing thoughts and tendencies to make rash decisions contributes to poor judgment. These racing thoughts can emotionally and mentally torment a double-minded person.

- Being easily swayed by others, without taking time to think through or take a stand on the issues one is being influenced with.

- Blame-shifting is a cause for indecision; it holds one back from taking responsibility. The person can in turn blame others for their ability to come to a decision. A double-minded person tends to over-rationalize or overthink a situation, to such a degree that they do not decide anything.

- Information junkie: Frequently seeking information or knowledge, but never acting on the information gained or provided the guidance.

- A double-minded person is faint-hearted; they frequently seek advice and are overly dependent on other people to make decisions. This state of indecision can predispose them to become trapped in abusive, manipulative, or exploitive relationships where they are taken advantage of. Such as person is a target and at high risk for victimization by people with wrong intentions.

- A double- minded person prefers quick fixes and shortcuts. They are unwilling to seek God's direction or patiently wait for the answer. Such a person will revert to old patterns of behavior when challenged or seek former unsavory friends for counsel.

- Unstable relationships, temporary employment, and lack of commitment or loyalty mark the life a double-minded. They are unreliable and cannot be trusted to complete a task or follow through on their spoken word. They tend to be loners or associate with people they can control.

- They are inconsistency and unstable in spiritual matters, including prayer, devotions, Bible reading, and fasting. Fellowship with other believers is scant; church attendance is haphazard, at best.

Double-mindedness can result from trauma, mostly when there was pressure to perform; the victim was always criticized, no matter how well they executed a task. They feel like every effort is doomed to fail before they even begin. They hesitate to make decisions for fear of punishment. They feel like they were never able to do anything right. Such a person may resort to inaction.

Double-mindedness can also be a generational issue; a false belief transmitted through the bloodline. Such beliefs can be as simple as saying, "I never make good choices"; this is also called a word curse. The person thinks they cannot make appropriate decisions, so they pass the responsibility on to someone else instead of taking the initiative. They make poor decisions; or refuse make any decision.

Because double-mindedness stalls destiny, it should be dealt with through fervent deliverance prayer, to break the stronghold. Below is a sample prayer that you can use. By faith, pray this prayer and be set free, permanently, in Jesus' Name:

> *Father, in the Name of Jesus, I thank you that the life I now live is through Jesus Christ, who died for me. With Christ in me, I also have the mind of Christ. I thank you for the assurance that Jesus was crucified and chastised for my freedom. Therefore, in the Name of Jesus, I repent of double-mindedness and renounce anything I have done*

*to entertain these thoughts. I repent of any covenants and legal rights I have given in these thoughts and dissolve them in the Name of Jesus Christ. I cleanse my mind by the blood of Jesus, and I close all doors that may have allowed stronghold and the spirit of double-mindedness to operate in my life. Lord Jesus, I renounce double-mindedness; I break the stronghold of double-mindedness by the blood of Jesus, and in the Name of Jesus, I command the stronghold to be broken.*

*I separate myself from indecision, anxiety, fear, confusion, racing thoughts, passivity, trauma, genetic perfectionism, and generational causes. I command these spirits and tendencies to go out of my mind, spirit, and body in Jesus's Name. By the Blood of Jesus and in the Name of Jesus, I uproot every cause and origin of double-mindedness in my life, including those from my bloodline on my paternal and maternal side. I declare all strongholds of double-mindedness are broken and made permanently ineffective, in Jesus's name. I command the demons and familiar spirits responsible for double-mindedness to go out of my life, in the name of Jesus. I thank you, Lord, for my freedom. I declare that I have the mind of Christ. I declare that I have peace, joy, righteousness, and a sound mind in Jesus's Name. I declare sound judgment and the ability to make good and right decisions from this day forward. I welcome progress into my life. Lord, fill me and empower me with your Spirit to accomplish every detail of my destiny according to the plans that you have for me, from this day on. In Jesus Name, I pray. Amen!*

Hallelujah! You are free! Start making right decisions from now on. Begin with a list of simple tasks and check them off as you complete them. Celebrate each accomplishment, no matter how small, then proceed gradually to setting more significant objectives. Fill your mind with promises of God concerning your destiny. Consider repeating the following declaration (out loud) regularly, especially at the beginning of each day: *"I am created in the image of God, and I have the mind of Christ. God has given me the Spirit of power, love, and a sound mind. This enables me to do everything through Christ, who strengthens me. Holy Spirit, help me make good decisions and accomplish each task today in the name of Jesus!"* The Scriptures associated with this set of declarations are Genesis 1:26-27; 1 Corinthians 2:16; 2 Timothy 1:7; John 14:15-18; Acts 1:8; James 1:5; and Philippians 4:13.

## Unhealthy Relationships

There are five relational needs that each human being strives for: love, belonging, acceptance, security, and affirmation. I must admit I was very naïve in relational matters. I was too trusting; I had no models of healthy relationships to instruct me; I believed that anyone who professed to be a Christian was a true Christian. I took people at their word because that is the way I am. Despite my backslidden state, I still believed in treating others as I would expect to be treated. I assumed that all Christians would walk in integrity, conduct themselves as persons of honor, and keep their word. I was shocked, though, to learn that some of the most untrustworthy people professed Christianity.

I began to see a pattern of behavior in the people I befriended: they had no good intentions! This doubtful behavior was evident, not only in romantic relationships but also in casual friendships. Most people befriended me to get what they needed, and then they would disappear. I noticed, too, that I became the kind of friend who could be counted on to assist in these people's emergencies, but I was not included in their social activities. I tell you; I have had my share of betrayals, hurts, and disappointments. I thank God for His mercy in healing and restoring me to a healthy self-respecting identity, and also for giving me the ability to set boundaries. If so-called friends or acquaintances have ever betrayed you, I encourage you to forgive them, release the trauma of those negative experiences, and let God comfort and avenge you. God assures us of His vindication, *"repay no one evil for evil. Have regard for good things in the sight of all men. If it is possible, as much as depends on you, live peaceably with all men. Beloved do not avenge yourselves, but rather give place to wrath; for it is written, "Vengeance is Mine, I will repay," says the Lord." Romans 12: 17-19, NKJ.*

As a single woman, I struggled to understand the characteristics of a satisfying, godly marriage relationship because I had no healthy relationship as an example then. I had a twisted definition of a suitable mate. In my carnal thinking, my idea of an ideal mate defined by specific standards that were less than godly. I suffered through four relationships; in one of them, I remained engaged for four years without ever getting married. Every time, I justified sex before marriage, but it was just fornication under the guise of cohabitation and hope for marriage. The primary lie that accompanied cohabitation was, "this is an understandable practice, especially in a foreign country." The other lie was that God understood the financial challenges of living alone; cohabitation would cut down costs and help save money for the wedding; plus other believers are cohabitating-everyone is doing it! I knew I was pretty far gone at that point because I had lowered my standards, often compromising, to appease the men I dated. These are the effects of a reprobate, self-reliant mind. And even worse, I blatantly disobeyed God. The most damning conviction that I have since repented of was engaging in fornication, and then serving in church the next day, unrepentantly as though everything was fine. The men I dated often accompanied me to church; we were all professing Christians! Thank God for His mercies and loving-kindness! After rededicating my life, I committed to remaining pure until God sends me His handpicked mate.

Sometimes relational setbacks are demonically orchestrated. Satan can use extramarital sexual intercourse to transfer demonic spirits, which afflict and oppress. These are often a result of past generational sexual sins and demonically-inspired covenants, pacts, or trades established or transferred through idolatry. Such covenants get reinforced through avenues like sex with multiple partners, adultery, fornication, rape, molestation, and sometimes sexual assaults by demons, in which people report dreaming about having sexual intercourse with people or beings they cannot identify. People who are impacted by demonic sexual encounters often have difficulty getting married or maintaining a marriage or any other healthy relationship or conceiving children if they do not seek deliverance. Also, there could be a history of other types of setbacks in their live. I have examined this topic in my book, [9]Victorious Overcomer.

Spirits attract people with similar traits. Familiar spirits and victim spirits can sense and attract their targets. This scenario is how I sometimes ended up with a predator: a so-called friend, who was only after what I had to give, and then they disappeared. Promiscuous spirits attract too; life void of God makes one an open target to any demonic attack. To avoid such attacks, stay connected to Christ, submit to God, resist the devil, and he will flee. Draw near to God, and He will draw near to you. I recommend reading or watching teachings on the subject of the victim spirit by Arthur Burk.

Given the information above, should we seek God for relationships? The answer is yes! The writer of Proverbs teaches that *"the righteous choose their friends carefully, but the way of the wicked leads them astray,"* Proverbs 12:26, NIV. We can ask God to safeguard us and connect us with God-fearing, right-minded people. Wise and successful people surround themselves with others who are more successful than they are. We can

---

[9] (Adongo, 2020) Adongo, Pauline *Victorious Overcomer, Prayers and Declarations of Spiritual Warfare* (2020)

guard ourselves by associating with those who are mature and more knowledgeable. Young people can significantly benefit from spending some time with godly adults or experts in the industries or vocations they want to advance. Each person in a relationship has something to offer, and the offer should edify or encourage the other person. Next, we should ask God to show us how to honor the other person and protect the relationship. Some relationships are temporary, some are long-term, and some are covenantal; each type has its place. Lastly, concerning marriage, God intended that spouses complement one another in accomplishing the destiny God designed for their marriage. If you are married, ask God to show you your contribution to the success of your joint destiny. If you are single, ask God for a mate who you will jointly work with to accomplish God's destiny for your marriage.

## Recurrent Sickness

During the season of my backslidden life, I frequently suffered sudden bouts of unexplained, short-term physical discomfort and pain. The symptoms ranged from mild to severe: sinus and throat infections, generalized malaise, tension headaches, severe bowel irregularities, including Irritable Bowel Syndrome (IBS), fevers, and tiredness. Initially, I assumed they were symptoms commonly associated with seasonal weather changes or work-related stress. I even underwent a colonoscopy, which, for my age, was unusual, but the symptoms were severe enough to warrant it. The result of the colonoscopy was negative; nothing was wrong with me. The anxiety, fear, worry, and insecurity were the actual causes of the physical symptoms. The mind and body are closely integrated more than some are aware. But I also realized that I could have opened doors for demonic oppression through entertaining negative emotions.

Shortly after rededicating my life to God, I discerned that some of these symptoms were demonic attacks, especially the frequent sinus and throat infections. One evening, when an infection afflicted me, I called a friend, and we prayed together, canceling the demonic attack; I got delivered from them. Since then, I resolved to be vigilant through prayer; and fasting where needed; against all attacks of the enemy: *"Thanks be to God, who always gives us the victory through His Son Jesus Christ!". 1 Corinthians 15:57, NASB.*

## Reinforcing Generational Curses

As discussed, my past incidences of confusion led to poor judgment and destructive behaviors. With my thinking processes muddled, I had trouble making rational decisions. Because I was not confident in my identity, I engaged in harmful habits to mask my fears, and insecurities, and numb my pain. I have since learned that confusion is a tool the enemy uses to launch attacks.

I discovered that I exhibited strange behaviors that were out-of-character for me. One example was excessive shopping and reckless spending that frequently left me broke. Poverty is a curse of satan; a lack of discipline in finances could be an earmark of satan's schemes. My advice is to watch out for unusual habits that suddenly spring up. Other destructive habits, such as promiscuity, fornication, or addictions of any kind often affect young adults. In a world of too much freedom and accommodation, believers need to be alert and separate themselves from immorality. Satan often destroys people by enticing and tempting them with counterfeit solutions and ungodly outlets for their unfulfilled desires.

Generational curses remain active when not recognized and resolved. Curses are often passed on through the same means of entry to the person they first affected. So if a curse were initiated through stealing, it would likely be passed along through theft or extortion. If a curse were initiated by anger, it would probably be transferred through a temptation that will result in anger. If a curse were initiated through sexual interaction, it would likely transferred sexually. Sexual intercourse is a covenant; when people engage in sex, they basically covenant with what is in one another. Generational curses and evil spirits are transferred in this manner. This among others is a good reason to refrain from premarital sex; and to break soul ties from past relationships before getting married. One way of overcoming generational curses is to keep the doors through which they transferred permanently closed.

I have learned that satan afflicts when a person is at the peak of rebellion and or when they are exhausted, depressed, or discouraged. He often targets when we have let our guards down when we are emotionally, physically, or mentally vulnerable. So we must stay alert and ensure all doors are closed. You can identify curses based on the negative tendencies that you observe in your family. Should you sense that you are lured towards those tendencies, then it is likely that a curse is being transferred. But thank God for His mercies, curses were broken at the cross, and each believer has the power to destroy them utterly.

## Financial Setbacks

Following my restoration, I reminisced about the many hard lessons I learned during my backslidden life. Just one mistake can cause a ripple effect; the enemy only needed one open the door to inflict damage upon other aspects of my life. Almost all areas of my life were affected, but not to the same degree. Finances seemed to be a vulnerable spot. Satan never plays fair; he comes to steal, kill, and destroy. When I removed God from my contact list, the enemy took advantage of potential points of access. That is why we must commit all areas to God, not just one or two specific areas.

My utmost area of concern was financial security. Consequently, this area was fiercest struggle, but the underlying demonic spirit of poverty intensified this battle even more. Over that period, whenever I tried to save money, there always seemed to be a situation that demanded more. I experienced unexpected personal and family emergencies that required finances; there were mysterious, sudden vehicle and appliance breakdowns, and extreme stress at work, which often left me exhausted when I returned home. I remember sleeping on the couch, on several occasions, because I did not have the energy to walk to my bedroom.

While not all financial issues are connected to the spirit of poverty, some challenges can also result from poor financial planning, lack of investment knowledge, living without a budget, or setting unrealistic financial goals. Other unwise habits, like excessive shopping, living beyond your means, choosing unstable investments, or supporting overdependent people, can also contribute to poverty.

The section below lists the signs of a poverty spirit. Awareness of these will help you recognize and overcome them. According to Dr. Dave Williams, **The spirit of poverty:** puts blinders over believer's eyes; puts fear in the hearts of believers; steals ambition; makes dreams seem impossible; tears you down by reminding you of past failures; makes one feel less qualified than others; drives one into the back rows of life; convinces you that the biggest win would be to keep from losing; twists Scriptures about money, wealth, greed, and covetousness. The spirit of poverty often attracts lack, decrease, debt, loss, hardship, scarcity, and shortages; it works through the stages of a poverty mentality; thoughts, beliefs, and addiction, before it becomes a stronghold: (Charisma Magazine: Williams D, 2017; *7 Discernible Signs the Spirit of Poverty Is Attacking You.*) https://www. charismamag.com/spirit/spiritual-warfare/33370-7-discernible-signs-the-spirit-of-poverty-is-attacking-you

Other signs of a poverty spirit include:

- constant fear and worry about finances that makes one either overspend or be frugal,

- tendencies to engage in get-rich-quick schemes, such as Ponzi or Pyramid schemes,

- lack of contentment or appreciation with what you have,

- always seeking more; or on the contrary, hoarding, based on fear of losing what you have

- covetousness-envying what others have

- unhealthy competition,

- overworking; manipulating others for compensation or advancement in a business or job opportunity

- scheming with others to gain more wealth,

- excessive shopping or unnecessarily living within a strict budget

- tend to brag and show off wealth as a form of superiority over others

- history of unresolved debt, always borrowing, but not repaying,

- instability in jobs or business

- always exploring new ventures that never succeed,

- prone to extortion, theft, or robbery

- tend to criticize anything that is prosperous or powerful

- settling for any job offer as long as it pays better than the last one,

- constant worry, and sleepless nights worrying about money

- inability to work for free

- inconsistencies in tithing or giving to your church or not giving at all

- believing that God blesses others, but not you

- being jealous when others are blessed

- difficulty giving in church or helping others

- when personal leisure expenditure outweighs what you give in church

- excessive focus on cheap bargains instead of purchasing quality new items

- having a mindset of, "I can't afford that," "I don't have enough money," or "that is for rich people."

- barely making ends meet from regularly money earned

True identity is lost when more value is placed on materialism, such as: following the latest fad, measuring success by income level, valuing possessions over relationships with God and people, and defining significance by accumulated possessions. As born-again believers, we are not defined by what we have or do not have. Our true identity is in our Lord Jesus Christ.

Finances can also be negatively impacted when we fail to tithe, give tithes in the wrong place or with the wrong motive. I learned this lesson the hard way. We should give obediently out of love, not giving to receive, but rather approaching the acts of giving, tithing, and benevolence from a heart of worship love, and thanksgiving to God. I have also learned not to buy a blessing; such practices often stem from wrong motives of greed instead of enhancing God's purposes. Do not be manipulated to give to receive a blessing, a prophecy, or a breakthrough in prayer. Honoring and blessing God's ministers is good; but we should wisely guard against manipulation of resources and time, carefully discerning the "soil" where we sow. Any tithe, offering, or service to God is a seed. Healthy seeds, when sown in healthy environments, will result in fruitfulness, multiplication, and a great harvest. The return on the investment is here on earth, and also in heaven. Anything offered to God in love has excellent returns!

True and eternal prosperity is in Jesus Christ. No amount of money or wealth can satisfy. Wealth can undoubtedly provide a degree of comfort, but total satisfaction is in our Lord Jesus Christ. Psalm 121 remains a personal favorite that I frequently reflect on; consider revisiting it when overwhelmed with any need, including finances. This psalm begins with, *"I lift up my eyes to the hills. From where does my help come? My help comes from the Lord, who made heaven and earth. He will not let your foot be moved; he who keeps you will not slumber. Behold, he who keeps Israel will neither slumber nor sleep. The Lord is your keeper; the Lord is your shade on your right hand. The sun shall not strike you by day, nor the moon by night. The Lord will keep you from all evil; he will keep your life. The Lord will keep your going out and your coming in from this time forth and forevermore"*, *Psalm 121, NKJV.* Trust God for your provision; always thank Him for what you already have.

## Comparison and Envy

The quest for success and independence can divert focus away from the essential matters in life. When one fails to trust God for provision, the result of comparison with others and coveting what they have can be very damaging because one does not know how they acquired what they have. Some have obtained their wealth from an inheritance or through sincere hard work; others may have obtained wealth through evil and dubious means. Healthy competition is a much better means of evaluation. Healthy competition should motivate us to do exceedingly better and to help those struggling maximize their potential.

Comparison is unhealthy because it often leads to compromise. I once succumbed to the pitfall of compromise when I tried to fit in with others whose opinions and approval seemed important. I had not comprehended my true identity, and I ended up downplaying my beliefs in a bid for acceptance. The Bible warns that we are not to be unequally yoked with unbelievers or believers with questionable behaviors. We should be imitators of God, not the world; (see 2 Corinthians 6:14 and Ephesians 5: 1). Compromise, in my case, led to misery and exploitation by so-called friend. People even marry wrong mates when they comprise God's standards and their personal values. I fell victim to financial, psychological, and spiritual exploitation and abuse due to association with the wrong crowd. My desire for what others possessed resulted in my settling for less than what God intended for me. I should clarify here that I desired friendship and company like those around me; that was the bait of the comparison I entertained. Howbeit I ended up in the wrong company of acquaintances.

At times comparison masks pain and loneliness or the need for affirmation or comfort. For example, in a group, a neglected person may live or dress extravagantly to be like the person receiving the attention. A desire to attain what others have, be accepted, or have a sense of belonging, exposes a much deeper issue that needs to be addressed. Such a view can cause financial stress or loss if the void is filled with materialism. Living above your means for the sake of acceptance only provides temporary gratification, and often devastates, if rejected despite their best efforts to impress or belong. I observed, in my backslidden years, the influx of young adults in my circle, who purchased expensive vehicles and got married because their peers were doing so. I was sad to hear later of the increase in divorce-rates of people who married for the wrong reasons and the drama associated with the competition. Let me end this section by warning about social media! Social media plays a huge role in luring people to false identity- what other people post does not necessarily reflect the truth. We should be discerning and selective with the information we embrace on social media!

The writer of Proverbs says, *"do not let your heart envy sinners, but always be zealous for fear of the Lord all day,"* Proverbs 23:17-18, NKJV. Happiness is contentment with what we have while we work towards more important things. Appreciation, joy, and empowerment ensue from what we genuinely work toward; whereas anything acquired prematurely or hastily inflicts unnecessary stress. Comparison reflects insecurity and unbelief. Each person is uniquely created with a specific destiny. Comparison denies us the ability to maximize our efforts and focus on the destiny God designed for us. Comparison, then, equates to living a strained, empty life, since we would be living a destiny that was not intended for us. Most aspects of life require patience, hard work, and then more patience. God provides every need according to His riches in glory. To the righteous, God does not withhold any good thing. Hard work, useful information, understanding, wisdom, and patience will eventually result in immense productivity. God is faithful to meet every need. He makes all things beautiful in His time (see Ecclesiastes 3:11).

## Mental and Emotional Instability

A preexisting mental or emotional condition can exacerbate new psychological conditions. I did not know that our family was affected by anything like this. But when I decided to interview relatives, I learned that we had a background of generational depression, anxiety, and suicide. Discovery of these root causes opened the door of deliverance, and I was easily set free.

Because I was trying so hard to make my life mean something apart from God, I endured several setbacks; I had health issues due to stress, I suffered rejection, and experienced painful relational breakups. There was a time that I was so depressed I took prescription medication to manage the depression. I was involved in a series of relationships; in each one, I was always hopeful that it would result in marriage, but that did not happen. I contemplated suicide three times. One was from being overwhelmed with family responsibilities, and the other two incidences were because of failed relationships.

Bouts of anger accompanied the depression. I had exceptionally low tolerance in many areas. Until my deliverance in 2014, I was extremely strict, highly principled, and blatant, which frequently sounded harsh! I was very much a perfectionist in most things. The bulk of the anger was triggered by family issues, and occasionally, by work situations, though I tried not to let work issues to get me-that was one my values. I am mostly an introvert. When I get offended, I initially suppress my reactions, but then at the last straw, I can blow up and be very harsh and blunt in my responses. Most of the anger arose because I felt I was not being heard or respected. Also, as the eldest sister, guiding my siblings was such a challenge at times. When they ignored my counsel, I became outraged, because often I would have to be the one to help them out of their avoidable predicament. With time, I learned to set boundaries and allow them to learn from their mistakes. I have also learned that I am not responsible for everyone- I only need to engage with and support those God wants me to help. I have learned that I was not created put out every fire; now, I would rather wait to be consulted for advice.

Besides suffering from depression and ager, I was in constant fear of the future. I had no one to confide in for support; thus, I was always consumed with worry and anxiety about my financial security. I believed the lie that my prospects would be secure if I married a highly professional man. I even wrote this requirement in my prayer-list for a husband. I laid out qualities such as "must have a master's degree, lawyer or medical doctor preferred, etc." I reasoned that such professions would provide the financial security I desired, but I later discarded that list, following my rededication to Jesus Christ. Again, there is nothing wrong with being specific in prayer; but clearly, my prayer list was fear-based.

I sought advanced education in an attempt to secure my future and enjoy a sense of accomplishment. I very stringently set goals and tried to make sure I achieved each objective. Goals were essential to me since my childhood. But, as I became an adult, the stakes were higher. When I failed to meet my objectives, I would get outraged, and then the anger would later degenerate into depression, a sense of failure, and fear of impending doom. Emotionally, I vacillated from one mood to another. Sometimes I was adventurous. I would take risks (sometimes high risks), or else I would retreat into passivity. In this subdued state, I made regrettable and costly emotional decisions.

Intense anger often masks deep, underlying pain. My coping mechanism since childhood was to repress and compartmentalize my emotions when I was faced with challenges, trauma, or abuse. I suppressed anger in my subconscious, so the cries of helplessness were released through the escape valve of rage. I also think the anger was partly due to a generational issue that needed resolution. In deliverance ministry, wisdom is required to explore all areas and resolve everything to ensure complete deliverance. If you have a history similar to mine, or if there are past issues that you have suppressed or ignored, the problem could be generational. If anyone suffers from depression, anger, fear, or suicidal tendencies, the problem could be from suppressed trauma. Jesus Christ wants to set everyone free from all bondage. Through the cross, He set captives free. All we need to do is to accept our freedom by breaking agreement with these generational strongholds. Isaiah says, *"He (Jesus Christ) was wounded for our transgressions and bruised for our iniquities,"* Isaiah 53:5, KJV. Generational sins and traits often link to iniquities. I have repented on behalf of my ancestors, renounced the iniquities of alcoholism and anger, and I was set free from anger! This same freedom-experience is available right now for every believer in Jesus' Name!

God's power to break bondages and bring restoration through Jesus Christ is revealed in the entire chapter of Isaiah 61. This Scripture is about healing, restoration, and recompense. Jesus says, *"the Spirit of the Lord God is upon Me (Jesus Christ) because the Lord has anointed Me to bring good news to the poor; He has sent me to bind up the brokenhearted, to proclaim liberty to the captives, and the opening of the prison to those who are bound; to proclaim the year of the Lord's favor, and the day of vengeance of our God; to comfort all who mourn; to grant to those who mourn in Zion- to give them a beautiful headdress instead of ashes, the oil of gladness instead of mourning, the garment of praise instead of a faint spirit, that they may be called oaks of righteousness, the planting of the Lord, that he may be glorified,"* Isaiah 61:1-3,ESV. Most believers are familiar with the idea of asking God for our daily bread in the Lord's prayer, but deliverance and freedom are the bread of the righteous, as well, (see Matthew 15:21-28) God desires that each of us would be set free from the prisons of depression, anger, worry, anxiety, and fear.

Our salvation also includes deliverance. This promise is available in Joel 2:32, ESV: *"It shall come to pass that everyone who calls on the name of the Lord shall be saved. For in Mount Zion and Jerusalem, there shall be those who escape, as the Lord has said, and among the survivors shall be those whom the Lord calls".* The meaning of the word "salvation," takes in three concepts: saved, healed, and delivered. All that is required is to ask! Isaiah 53:5 captures the full package of our salvation rendered, forgiveness of sin, freedom from bondage, deliverance, and physical and emotional healing. The power of

God's promises is that they never change; they are current and applicable to our present situations.

As previously shared, unbelief was a critical, underlying factor in my efforts to be self-reliant. Unbelief is the absence of trust; unbelief causes fear, anxiety, and worry. I did not believe that God would come through for me, so I took matters into my own hands. However, Jesus assures us of His provision and protection of all creation including human beings. See His promise in the Gospel of Luke, *"And he said to his disciples, 'Therefore I tell you, do not be anxious about your life, what you will eat, nor about your body, what you will put on. For life is more than food and the body more than clothing. Consider the ravens: they neither sow nor reap, they have neither storehouse nor barn, yet God feeds them. Of how much more value are you than the birds! And which of you, by being anxious, can add a single hour to his span of life. If then you are not able to do as small a thing as that, why are you anxious about the rest? Consider the lilies, how they grow: they neither toil nor spin, yet I tell you, even Solomon in all his glory was not arrayed like one of these. But if God so clothes the grass, which is alive in the field today, and tomorrow is thrown into the oven, how much more will he clothe you, O you of little faith! And do not seek what you are to eat and what you are to drink, nor be worried. For all the nations of the world seek after these things, and your Father knows that you need them. Instead, seek His kingdom, and these things will be added to you'"* Luke 12:22-31, ESV.

The prayer of petition is another key to combat anxiety and worry. Jesus assures us of God's response when we ask. He says, *"Ask, and it will be given to you; seek, and you will find; knock, and it will be opened to you. For everyone who asks receives, and the one who seeks finds, and to the one who knocks it will be opened Or which one of you, if his son asks him for bread, will give him a stone? Or if he asks for a fish, will give him a serpent? If you then, who are evil, know how to give good gifts to your children, how much more will your Father who is in heaven give good things to those who ask him"!* Matthew 7:7-11 ESV. The apostle Paul also encourages us that; *"we should not be anxious for anything, but in everything by prayer and supplication, with thanksgiving, let your requests be made known to God; and the peace of God, which surpasses all understanding, will guard your hearts and minds through Christ Jesus, Philippians 4:6, NKJV.* Also, Psalm 55:22 and 1 Peter 1:7; both encourage us to cast our cares on the Lord. He will sustain us; he will never let the righteous be shaken.

The last point about fear: God assures us that He will guide us through life, *"I will instruct you and teach you in the way you should go; I will guide you with My eye. Do not be like the horse or like the mule, which have no understanding, which must be harnessed with bit and bridle, or else they will not come near you", Psalm 32:8-9, NIV.* In another promise God assures that He will be with us through the journey. He says, *"have I not commanded you? Be strong and courageous. Do not be afraid; do not be discouraged; for the Lord, your God will be with you wherever you go," Joshua 1:9, NIV.*

My deliverance occurred on an evening after returning home from work when I felt drawn to pray in my living room. I began by praying in tongues or the language of the Holy Spirit. As I prayed, I could sense that the Holy Spirit was praying so aggressively that I later screamed. I knew something remarkable happened at that moment, but I did not grasp the full impact of what had transpired until the next morning when I drove to work. Most of my reflections and part of my daily devotions happen as I am driving. That morning, I tried to revisit my depressive issues, but I could not! Instead, I was filled with joy and the desire to dance! I received the Spirit of Joy! The joy of the Lord is our strength. My season of ashes and mourning ended—instead, the oil of joy and the garment of praise adorned my heart. God crowned me with beauty. This is a magnificent testimony because when I was depressed, I "wore the depression" like a garment or mask; the despondency would even darken my countenance and affect my demeanor. But I am a testimony of God's restorative power because I am walking in my righteous identity as His child, I am rooted in Christ, and I display His mighty joyous splendor across the earth! Hallelujah, Jesus Christ, be magnified!

# CHAPTER FIVE

# THE ALTERNATIVE PLAN

The writer of Psalm 139 indicates that each person has a preordained plan in a book that contains the number of days that should be fulfilled by each person here on earth. God foreknew us, predestined, and established our identity while still in our mothers' wombs. At birth, God already knew our destinies. King David says, *"my frame was not hidden from you when I was being made in secret, intricately woven in the depths of the earth. Your eyes saw my unformed substance; in your book were written, every one of them, the days that were formed for me, when as yet there was none of them", Psalm 139:15-16, ESV.* There is further affirmation of our predestination in Ephesians 1:3-7, ESV which says *"blessed be the God and Father of our Lord Jesus Christ, who has blessed us in Christ with every spiritual blessing in the heavenly places, even as he chose us in him before the foundation of the world, that we should be holy and blameless before him. In love, he predestined us] for adoption to himself as sons through Jesus Christ, according to the purpose of his will, to the praise of his glorious grace, with which he has blessed us in the Beloved"* According to these Scriptures, our predestination was not only to live blameless lives but to live out the plans of that predestined life.

Knowledge of our predestination and a new identity in Christ is reassuring. God chose each of us before the foundations of the earth; through the redemptive power of the blood of Jesus Christ, we have been adopted as sons and daughters and restored to the original fellowship God had for us. Through that adoption, we can successfully live out the plans that God has for us. God strategically outlined this when He formulated each person's plans, saying, *"For I know the plans I have for you," declares the* LORD, *"plans to prosper you and not to harm you, plans to give you hope and a future," Jeremiah 29:11, NIV.* The Lord proceeds to assure us that, *"then you will call upon Me and go and pray to Me, and I will listen to you. And you will seek Me and find Me when you search for Me with all your heart. I will be found by you, says the Lord, and I will bring you back from your captivity; I will gather you from all the nations and from all the places where I have driven you, says the Lord, and I will bring you to the place from which I caused you to be carried away captive", Jeremiah 29:12-14, NIV.*

God's plan for your life remains unchanged no matter how many mistakes you have made or how much you have messed up. God can still realign your life to fit the plan He intended for you. Granted, there are consequences to everything we do; some are positive; others are negative. Most consequences, whether good or bad, have long term effects; but what God established for us remains unchanged. This is God's faithfulness in action. God is merciful, kind, and loving. Through His mercy and love, we can still connect to that original plan. Repentance draws us close to God, not away from Him. We repent out of our love and reverence to God because He also first loved us. Repentance is valuable. Repentance is the door to restitution of the original plan God created for each human.

God's plans include vital elements from Jeremiah 29:11-14. First, His plans are good, not evil; secondly, God plans to give us hope and a future. Thirdly, God reveals and executes His plans for restoration.

## God Values each Person

There is a frequently repeated pronouncement at the beginning of the book of Genesis, where God created the earth, and later, human beings. After creating each species, we see this statement *"God saw that it was good." Genesis 1: 10, KJV.* Later, when God created man and woman, He was pleased with His creation. *"Everything God does is perfect- as for God, his way is perfect: The Lord's word is flawless; He shields all who take refuge in him"*, Psalm 18:30, NKJV. Be assured that God values you since He created you. He also thinks highly of you because He created you in His image.

I struggled, for a long time, to believe that God loved me. I thought that my distressing experiences happened because I was not doing enough to be right with God. I continued to entertain this notion even after re-dedicating my life to Jesus Christ in 2009. One mid-morning, while standing at my dining table, I looked at the mirror and commented, "Pauline, you are beautiful," and I heard the Lord reply, saying, "and you are so loved, you are the beloved of God." Many changes stemmed from that moment. I was immediately able to embrace my identity as "Beloved," and I have continued to walk in the fullness of that name to date. I know that I am accepted, loved, and valued. I know that God smiles at me and that He is for me, all the time. This is the identity of my predestination. Zephaniah says, *"the Lord your God is with you, the Mighty Warrior who saves. He will take great delight in you; in His love, He will no longer rebuke you but will rejoice over you with singing"*, Zephaniah 3:17 NIV. God has happy thoughts of you and me! He rejoices over the righteous by singing songs of deliverance!

Each born-again believer was predestined by God to be saved. [10]Predestination simply means "determined beforehand, "to foreordain," or "destiny by divine decree." God already established that you would be saved and set apart for Him. The Apostle Paul says, *"Blessed be the God and Father of our Lord Jesus Christ, who has blessed us with every spiritual blessing in the heavenly places in Christ, just as He chose us in Him before the foundation of the world, that we should be holy and without blame before Him in love, having predestined us to adoption as sons by Jesus Christ to Himself, according to the good pleasure of His will, to the praise of the glory of His grace, by which He]made us accepted in the Beloved,"* Ephesians 1:3-6, NKJV. God accepts us!

---

[10] https://www.thefreedictionary.com/

# God's Restorative Mercy

The complete chapter of Psalm 103 is my testimony. I reflect on this is the life-scripture that frequently because it speaks of God's mercy, loving-kindness, and power to restore backsliders like myself. As I read this Psalm believing, I receive assurance of a restored life without shame or guilt. The first five verses speak of forgiveness, healing, deliverance, and restoration. I continue to experience different levels of freedom in these four areas since I recommitted to God. The Psalm commences with, *"Bless the Lord, O my soul and all that is within me, bless His holy name! Bless the Lord, O my soul, and forget not all His benefits: Who forgives all your iniquities, Who heals all your diseases, Who redeems your life from destruction, Who crowns you with lovingkindness and tender mercies, Who satisfies your mouth with good things so that your youth is renewed like the eagle's"*, Psalm 103:1-5, NKJV. I preached my first sermon from this Psalm and Psalm 107.

God outlines further assurance of His mercies in these verses, *"The Lord is merciful and gracious, slow to anger, and abounding in mercy. He will not always strive with us, nor will He keep His anger forever. He has not dealt with us according to our sins nor punished us according to our iniquities. For as the heavens are high above the earth, so great is His mercy toward those who fear Him; far as the east is from the west, so far has He removed our transgressions from us. As a father pities his children, so the Lord pities those who fear Him. For He knows our frame; He remembers that we are dust,"* Psalm 103:8-14, NKJV. Surely God is not out to "get us." He desires that no one would perish, and He repeatedly forgives without bringing up our past sins. These are His thoughts towards us! When we submit to His redemptive mercy, He redirects us to the plans He designed and predestined for each of us.

Our God and Father is loving and merciful. The story of the prodigal son in Luke 15:11-32 comes to mind. I, too, left the comfort, security, provision, and love of God, my loving Father. But in the Scripture, no matter how far the son had wandered, the father celebrated His return. This is the true unfailing love of God, our Father. Regardless of how far we drift, God stands firm on His Word and His promises for us. His mercies are new every morning; His love is from everlasting to everlasting. He forgives and blots out our sins, never to remember them again! God is always there waiting, with arms wide open in anticipation of the return of that one prodigal. I was that prodigal whom God restored at seven in the morning in April 2009 while I attended a professional conference in Las Vegas, Nevada. God was with me in my luscious hotel suite where I knelt and rededicated my life to Jesus Christ. I was alone with Jesus, and God embraced me just as I was. He can do the same for you right now.

## Plans of Peace

When we accepted Jesus as Lord and Savior, we received Him and all His attributes. One of the names of Jesus is "Prince of Peace." Jesus resides in us as the Prince of Peace. We can live in this peace and know that we receive guidance, we are secure, and He sustains when we set our minds on Him. Isaiah says, *"You (God) will keep him in perfect peace, Whose mind is stayed on You Because he trusts in You,"* Isaiah 26:3, NKJV.

God always guides in peace because of that is how He lives in His Kingdom. The Apostle Paul describes God's Kingdom as a kingdom of peace, saying, *"for the kingdom of God is not eating and drinking, but righteousness and peace and joy in the Holy Spirit,"* Romans 14:17, NKJV. However, confusion, anxiety, worry, panic, fear, rush decisions or pressure, chaos, restlessness, contentions, arguments, and drama are not from God. We experience these things when we follow our plans and leave God out of them. Furthermore, since God's thoughts towards us are for peace, God's heart and intentions align with that peace. God never intends to harm. He disciplines, but the purpose of His discipline is always to improve and mature us. As citizens of that peaceful kingdom, let us be confident that His peace will lead and guard us.

Peace is undoubtedly a significant aspect of God's character and nature; a peaceful house or nation often experiences growth and prosperity. An atmosphere of peace often results in unity, collaboration, love, and productivity. Most people prefer to live in a peaceful environment or with peaceful people. No wonder Jesus came as the Prince of Peace, but He also left that peace with us before He ascended. Jesus said, *"My (Jesus's) peace I leave with you. My peace I give to you; not as the world gives, do I give you. Let not your heart be troubled, neither let it be afraid", John 14:27, NKJV.* We may look to material things, professional achievements, or fellow humans to bring us peace, but peace is a Person, the person of Jesus Christ. We can only be receive Him by having a relationship with God. If you are currently experiencing unrest or uncertainty in any area of life, ask the Holy Spirit to direct you to what you need to do to get rid of turmoil in your life and usher in true peace. Jesus Christ was chastised for our peace, according to Isaiah 53:5, so you can renounce and resist anything that robs you of peace. Jesus is our peace!

## Harmless Plans

There is a false belief that has been circulated by some who say that God sends harmful circumstances to born-again believers as punishment for sin. These same people believe that sickness, adversity, and lack are meant to humble and teach the believer. But Scripture contradicts such doctrines. God says that *"He will not always strive with us, nor will He keep His anger forever. He has not dealt with us according to our sins nor punished us according to our iniquities; far as the east is from the west, so far has He removed our transgressions from us", Psalm 103:9-12, NKJV.* When we genuinely repent, God forgives our sins and does not recall them. God is not vindictive, nor does He retaliate with adversities to teach us a lesson in response to our sins or rebellion. He always extends

His merciful hands, motivated by His desire that none may perish. *"When we confess our sins, God is faithful and just to forgive us our sins and to cleanse us from all unrighteousness,"* 1 John 1:9, NKJV.

Satan's primary objective is to steal, kill, and destroy. Through his deception, satan convinces people to blame God for misfortunes. By blaming God, satan continues to create havoc in the lives of believers. I perceived God as harsh when I was backslidden. I did not connect my adverse experiences with the devil's schemes to destroy me. I was deceived. I thought that my uncomfortable circumstances were not only the consequence of poor choices, but also were intended as God's judgment and punishment. While it is true that God executes judgment, He only does this after giving numerous opportunities for repentance. Then He leaves us to our desires, as mentioned in Romans 1:28, a scripture that I have elaborated on in previous chapters. The Bible details several accounts of people who suffered harm when they unrepentantly persisted in sin. Consider the people's behavior in Noah's days and examine Pharaoh's story when he declined to release the Israelites. Many kings of Israel turned to idolatry, and their rebellion led to Israel's seventy years of captivity. The following situations allow the potential for harm from Satan because they serve as entry points and legal grounds for Satan and demons to launch attacks:

- continual rebellion against God

- an unrepentant heart

- hardened heart towards God's instructions

- living contrary to God's Word

- ignoring warnings from the Holy Spirit

- grieving the Holy Spirit

- poor decisions or judgments

- persecution for doing the right things and also for doing wrong

- opposition and attack by satan

- bitterness

Remember that a life that is resistant to God is an open invitation to Satan's attacks. He is the enemy who wants to deflect and distort your destiny.

## The Pruning Process As Part of God's Plan

The pruning and transformation process God takes us through can seem detrimental at times; however, the goal of the pruning process is to strengthen us, mature us, and position us for greater humility, authority, and purpose. **Transformation:** [11]"a complete change in the appearance or character of something or someone, mainly, so that thing or person is improved: a thorough or dramatic change in form or appearance. Other words for transformation: modification, revision, or amendment, metamorphosis, transfiguration, remodeling, reshaping, reconstruction, redoing, a makeover, reordering, renewal, revamping, or overhaul.

God develops us through pruning. Consider the pruning, discipline, and refining process as a quality assurance (QA) or quality improvement (QI) process like those used in industry. The outcome of this QI process in the believer will be evident through humility, maturity, character, the fruit of repentance, and the measure of impact and influence. We can be transformed several ways through God's QI:

We are transformed through the renewal of our minds by the word of God (Romans 12:2). The work of the Holy Spirit transforms us when we submit all areas of our lives to

---

[11] https://dictionary.cambridge.org/dictionary/english/transformation

Him- (Ephesians 4:23). We are sanctified by fleeing the works of the flesh. 2 Timothy indicates that *"in a great house there are not only vessels of gold and silver, but also of wood and clay, some for honor and some for dishonor. Therefore if anyone cleanses himself from the latter, he will be a vessel for honor, sanctified and useful for the Master, prepared for every good work. Flee also youthful lusts; but pursue righteousness, faith, love, peace with those who call on the Lord out of a pure heart"*, 2 Timothy 2:20-23, NKJV. Jesus says, *"I am the true vine, and My Father is the vinedresser. Every branch in Me that does not bear fruit He takes away, and every branch that bears fruit He prunes, that it may bear more fruit"* John 15:1-2, NIV. We are pruned and transformed to be more effective and fruitful.

God's refining fire also transforms us through the testing of our faith, as we see in the example of Shadrack, Meshach, and Abednego in Daniel 3. Although an enemy instigated their trial, they stood firm, holding onto their faith. They knew God would deliver them, but they were also adamant that if God did not, they still would not bow to idols! We need this type of bravery and faith in times of adversity and testing. This scripture shows the firm stance that these three took; *"If we are thrown into the blazing furnace, the God we serve is able to deliver us from it, and He will deliver us from Your Majesty's hand. But even if He does not, we want you to know, Your Majesty, that we will not serve your gods or worship the image of gold you have set up,"* Daniel 3:17-18 NIV. We, too, should be equally determined to stand the tests of adversity and the tests of pruning and transformation until God's purposes are achieved.

Other examples of God's refining fire are in Zechariah and Malachi. God says that *"I will bring the one-third through the fire, will refine them as silver is refined, And test them as gold is tested. They will call on My name, And I will answer them. I will say, 'This is My people'; And each one will say, 'The Lord is my God.'"* Zechariah 13:9 NJKV. Malachi says, "but who can endure the day of His coming? And who can stand when He appears? For He is like a refiner's fire and like launderers' soap. He will sit as a refiner and a purifier of silver; He will purify the sons of Levi, And purge them as gold and silver, That they may offer the Lord an offering in righteousness", Malachi 3:2-3, NIV. May God find us to be a strong army of pure, holy vessels of righteousness that have withstood every fiery test for His glory!

The writer of Hebrews explains this maturing process much better, saying, *"and you have forgotten the exhortation which speaks to you as to sons My son, do not despise the chastening of the Lord nor be discouraged when he rebukes you; for whom the Lord loves He chastens and scourges every son whom He receives. If you endure chastening, God deals with you as with sons; for what son is there whom a father does not chasten? But if you are without chastening, of which all have become partakers, then you are illegitimate and not sons. Furthermore, we have had human fathers who corrected us, and we paid them respect. Shall we not much more readily be in subjection to the Father of spirits and live? For they indeed for a few days chastened us as seemed best to them, but He for our profit, that we may be partakers of His holiness. Now no chastening seems to be joyful for the present, but painful; nevertheless, afterward, it yields the peaceable fruit of righteousness to those who have been trained by it".* Hebrews 12:5-11, NJKV.

Hardship, discipline, and adversity were never intended to wipe us out utterly, but God uses them to instruct and train us for the better. God allows all things to work for good out of love since we are called for His purposes. God's thoughts toward us are always good!

## Plans for Hope

The Merriam Webster dictionary defines hope as a [12] desire with anticipation; to want something to happen or be true; to desire with expectation of obtainment or fulfillment. Hope is a feeling of expectation and desire for a certain thing to happen." Hope often comes with optimism, an expectation of positive

---

[12]  https://www.merriam-webster.com/dictionary/hope

things. Jesus Christ became our Hope when we accepted Him as Lord and Savior. By receiving Him, we surrendered to His Lordship by faith, believing that He intends only good for us. Hope and faith go hand in hand; our hope and faith are in God, the Author and Finisher of our salvation.

I am often encouraged by this verse, *"being confident of this, that he who began a good work in you will carry it on to completion until the day of Christ Jesus," Philippians 1:6 NIV.* God is determined to finish what He started in you. We see in the creation story in Genesis and throughout the Bible in numerous accounts how God ensures that every plan or task gets accomplished. The other encouragement in this Scripture is that God is with us through each stage of the plan He has for us. God sustains us by His Spirit when we are weak or discouraged, and He walks us through to attain the goal. Faith and hope increase when we know that God is at work; we cannot accomplish anything merely by personal effort. Success in the plans God has for us requires partnership with God. We need to work in partnership with Him in each area of life! We need patience and persistence as we follow through and accomplish every plan because God has promised never to leave or forsake us.

My faith and hope in God increase whenever I reassess previous accounts of the great things God has done in my life. When faced with adversities, I often reflect on past breakthroughs, answered prayers, victories, and the miraculous testimonies of what God did in my life, such as when He delivered from depression and suicide! Those are enough to sustain my hope in God. We overcome by the Blood of the Lamb and by the Word of our testimonies. Recount your history with the Lord frequently to keep your hope up. The entire chapter of Hebrews 11 is full of examples of those who walked by faith and hoped in the Lord; because they wholeheartedly trusted God, they were considered righteous men and women. Reflect on Hebrews 11 frequently; the entire book of Psalms is another excellent hope-booster!

Despite delays, hindrances, and opposition, God watches over His word to ensure that what He has declared comes to pass;(Matthew 24:35). We should be confident in this hope and count on every word God has said concerning us, despite everything that would seem to be contrary. We are to hope in God's mercies, love, and kindness that are new every morning. Trust God's goodness and compassion each day. Endure the process as you work with God on His plans for you. Praise God. Hope steadfastly in Him and expect something good. Here is a Psalm of encouragement: "*Why, my soul, are you downcast? Why so disturbed within me? Put your hope in God, for I will yet praise Him, My Savior, and my God*", Psalm 42:11, NIV.

## Plans to Give You a Future

Some names and attributes of God are "Ancient of Days," and "Alpha and Omega". These Names represent the God of forever, the God who holds time, but yet exists beyond time, He is the God of destinies! Daniel mentions the name "Ancient of Days" saying, "*I watched till thrones were put in place, and the Ancient of Days was seated; His garment was white as snow, and the hair of His head was like pure wool. His throne was a fiery flame, its wheels a burning fire; a fiery stream issued and came forth from before Him. A thousand thousands ministered to Him; ten thousand times ten thousand stood before Him. The court was seated, and the books were opened*". Daniel 7:9-10, NKJV. God as the Ancient of Days existed before time. He is the God of generations past. He is the God who predestined and wrote out our plans in His book. He is the Lord, who saw us when we were still invisible in our mothers' wombs. God already planned our lives before we were born. He can catapult anything from the past to align with our present and future, including the time or things you have lost. Trust God to align everything He intended for you. God will not withhold any good thing from you!

In the context of this chapter, Alpha and Omega represent the of process, the God who carries us along each stage of the plans

He has for us. He is the initiator and yet, the God Who sees even to the end of time. His name is *"The Alpha and the Omega, the Beginning, and the End," says the Lord, "who was and who is, and who is to come; the Almighty," Revelation 1:8, NKJV.* I often reflect on this aspect of God when I get restless and anxious about prayers that have not yet been answered. I find hope and assurance in knowing that God sees the end from the beginning and that He has already planned for all things to occur in His perfect timing. The seasons of waiting are the most challenging, especially when I feel I have accomplished all I need to do. But God is faithful to bring to pass what He promised just in time. All of God's promises are yes and amen to those who trust Him. 2 Corinthians 1:20, NKJV. God watches over His word to perform (Jeremiah 1:12). God does not speak empty words; what He planned or said must happen-His words are active, and they produce what they were sent to do; (Numbers 23:19).

God is in charge of all things. When God instructs us to do something, we may not see the end product of what He is doing. Nonetheless, we should still trust God, stay the course, and know that He will bring us to a perfect finish. There is hope that He who started a good work in us will bring it to completion, (Philippians 1:6.).

Regardless of where you are right now, trust God in the journey. Know that the Alpha and Omega is never too early or too late. Indeed, we can ask Him to hasten some things in our favor but remember that God is always on time - His timing is perfect. God says, *"...yet for the appointed time it hastens toward the goal, and it will not fail. Though it tarries, wait for it, for it will certainly come, it will not delay", Habakkuk 2:3 NASB.* I often reflect on the following Scriptures when I am anxious about an outcome. May these Scriptures encourage you, too, as you look forward to your future.

*Remember the things I have done in the past. For I alone am God! I am God, and there is none like me. Only I can tell you the future before it even happens. Everything I plan will come to pass, for I do whatever I wish." God is with us from the day we are born, with us in the process of life, and knows how everything will end. The NKJV translation says, "declaring the end from the beginning, and from ancient times things that are not yet done, saying, 'My counsel shall stand, and I will do all My pleasure, Isaiah 46:9-10, NLT.*

*And I am sure of this, that he who began a good work in you will bring it to completion at the day of Jesus Christ'. This promise assures us that God, as the author of our plans, will take care of every detail, to see it through for us. Hallelujah! Philippians 1:6, ESV.*

*I will instruct you and teach you in the way you should go; I will counsel you with my eye upon you. Psalm 32:8, ESV.*

I picture God taking our hand and leading us step by step, like a GPS (Global Positioning System) instructing us to "make a right," "make a U-turn," "slow down," or warning us at different times throughout our lives. God's eyes will always be upon us; Jesus Christ promised to be with us. He said, *"I will never leave you nor forsake you." Hebrews 13:5b, NKJV.*

## Plans to Prosper you

Prosperity is not defined by or limited to money or material possessions. God desires that we prosper and thrive in these four areas: spiritual, physical, emotional, and mental. God's idea of prosperity is all-encompassing. He wants us to flourish spiritually, in career and social life, finances and marriage, and ministry and business. God created each of us to exist in abundance; there are no failures in God's eyes!

According to the Merriam Webster dictionary, [13] prosperity means the condition of being successful or thriving, especially economic well-being." Prosperity involves fruitfulness and growth in whatever we do, and that includes financial wealth. The writer of the epistle of John assures us of God's desire that we prosper in all things, *"Beloved, I pray that you may prosper in all things and be in health, just as your soul prospers." 3 John 1:2, NKJV.* There is a connection, then, between our soul's health and the health of our minds, bodies, and finances. God's will for the prosperity of His children is also included in Psalms, which says, *"Let them shout for joy and be glad who favor my righteous cause; and let them say continually, Let the Lord be magnified, Who has pleasure in the prosperity of His servant." Psalm 35:27, NKJV.* God does not delight in suffering.

Real prosperity comes by relying on God while following and obeying His Word or commands. Real wealth comes from fully trusting the Lord and submitting everything Him. The first Psalm exemplified someone who walks in total abundance. *"Blessed is the one who does not walk in step with the wicked or stand in the way that sinners take or sit in the company of mockers, but whose delight is in the law of the Lord, and who meditates on his law day and night. That person is like a tree planted by streams of water, which yields its fruit in season and whose leaf does not wither—whatever they do prospers". Psalm 1:3 NIV.* Many of God's promises are conditional The provision for prosperity is that the righteous will not be unequally yoked with unbelievers. This inequality can compromise the believers' faith. We should pursue God's word and incorporate it daily as a lifestyle. If believers meet these conditions then; (a) they will continually be grounded, anchored, and unshakeable like a tree whose roots are held firm against adverse weather or circumstances. (b)They will continuously bear fruit; they earn profits, and gain incentives in the jobs or businesses, and there will be fruitful. Because the believer's walk and faith in God, such a person will never have a poor harvest from what they have sowed. They will be bountifully rewarded, meaning they

---

[13] Merriam Webster dictionary

will experience tremendous returns on their investments, and derive profitable outcomes. (c) They will have the ability to bear fruit always, in any season. Challenges do not bewilder them; they know that God will still come through for them, regardless of the obstacles. They will be productive nonetheless! This is faith at work! (d) The believer will prosper in all things! "Whatever" in this verse means anything that person engages in has God's approval for success, end of story! This broad concept is challenging to try to wrap our brains around. The possibilities are endless, but God has it all covered. Glory to His Name!

Based on God's attributes and character, we can approach every aspect of life, believing that God wants us to prosper. Whatever God has given us to do, He wants us to flourish, increase, prosper, and leave a legacy for future generations. Moreover, we are not alone in attaining this prosperity. God will provide helpers to support us in accomplishing these plans. The first Helper is the Holy Spirit, Who will teach, guide, counsel, and champion us according to John 14:15-18 and John 16:13-15. The next help is Angels; God sends them to assist us in all things. Angels support us in various capacities; *"Are not all angels ministering spirits sent to serve those who will inherit salvation?"* Hebrews 1:14, NIV. Take courage in the fact that we have a support system for our plans. God, Himself, will watch over us. By nature, He never fails; God will be with us throughout our life. Declare this Scripture over yourself often, especially if you feel you are too far gone to realign with God's plan. God gave this same promise to Jacob when He fled from Laban, saying; *behold, I am with you and will keep you wherever you go and will bring you back to this land; for I will not leave you until I have done what I have spoken to you,"* Genesis 28:15, NIV. Trust that God will be with you at each juncture of the plans He has for you.

God advances us progressively from one maturity level to another. We are continually growing; He wants us to walk in the fullness of His glory and power, reflecting Christ in us at all times. There was never any lack in Jesus' ministry. He supplied physical and spiritual needs. His first miracle provided wine at the wedding party, followed by healings, deliverances, resurrections, and even money to pay local taxes. Jesus multiplied food to feed large crowds that had gathered to listen to Him. He showed compassion to widows, children, and those with long-term suffering. Jesus prospered wherever He went, and He desires that for us, too, while we are still on earth.

The ministry of Jesus Christ is the implementation of the Kingdom of God on earth- the impact of that Kingdom releases substantial prosperity. As believers, we also have access and authority to live in the fullness of God's Kingdom. Our identity in Christ validates our standing with God because we are co-heirs with Christ. Let us continually pursue the goal of infusing our immediate surroundings with God's kingdom. Each born-again believer has the potential bring heaven to earth. Psalm 92 is a great way to end this chapter: *"the righteous shall flourish like a palm tree; He shall grow like a cedar in Lebanon. Those who are planted in the house of the Lord Shall flourish in the courts of our God. They shall still bear fruit in old age They shall be fresh and flourishing, to declare that the Lord is upright; He is my rock, and there is no unrighteousness in Him"*, *Psalm 92:12-15, NKJV.*

# CHAPTER SIX

# GOD HAS SUPPORT SYSTEMS FOR YOUR LIFE

God did not intend for us to live a life in solitude or isolation. He often included others in the fulfillment of most of His objectives. The Trinity, which encompasses God the Father, Son, and Holy Spirit, worked together in the initial plan to create the earth. We see this collaboration in the creation of Mankind; God said, "let Us-meaning the Trinity, make Man in Our image, (see Genesis 1:26 NIV). Then God saw fit to create Eve as a companion and helper so that Adam was not alone. Later on, in the deliverance of the Israelites, Moses had Aaron and Joshua to help him. King David had priests, prophets, and a fierce army during his reign. Finally, Jesus had disciples alongside Him whom He trained to implement His purpose on earth. Similarly, God has designated support systems for the plan He has for us through strategic connections.

## Strategic Connections

**God places strategic people in our lives to help us fulfill our destiny.** As we stay connected to Jesus and remain in His will, God will send the right people to support us. But if we shut God out, we will miss those appointments. Here is my testimony: While pursuing my first degree, God provided a student named Maridale, who had graduated ahead of me.

She gave me textbooks and uniforms for my practicum. After graduation, an executive leader gave me my first professional job as a registered nurse and later promoted me to a management position at age 26. While I was in that position, God sent a supervisor who coached me in leadership and management skills. I am still grateful for the coaching my supervisor provided. I have continued to utilize those skills throughout my profession in executive leadership and administration. As I pursued a second degree, another supervisor bought me books towards my baccalaureate degree and purchased graduation pins for the nursing degree I attained. Here, God placed three strategic ladies to support my healthcare administration career.

## A Testimony of Provision

I lived in a small efficiency apartment in Allentown, Pennsylvania, and desired a larger place than the one I rented. God worked through a classmate in my baccalaureate program to find me a better apartment. I moved into a one -bedroom in-law-suite with all amenities and lived in it for four years until my relocation to West Chester, Pennsylvania. The rent for the new apartment was much more reasonable. This enabled me to save money towards my tuition, and I was able to complete both the baccalaureate and attain a third-degree; an MBA in Healthcare Administration debt-free. I have other countless examples of unsolicited assistance from people in addition to the support of the Holy Spirit and angels in my life thus far!

The example above shows the connections God provided for me so I could pursue further education. You could be reading this and wondering if God would do the same for you. Whatever your situation, ask God to bring the people and resources you need to accomplish His will in your life. Jesus encourages us to ask in John 14:13-14 ESV, saying, *"whatever you ask in my name, this I will do, that the Father may be glorified in the Son. If you ask me anything in my name, I will do it".* Use this Scripture to ask God for the needs in your life.

Sometimes God will assign us to do things alone, but on other occasions, He requires partnerships with other people. We should pray to be connected with the right people for the season God has us in. Secondly, we should pray for increased wisdom, to discern when the season with people has ended. I once made the mistake of staying too long in one place. God directed me multiple times to leave within six months of attending a fellowship, but I stayed a year and a half. When I did leave, I was very hurt and broken. I later realized that my mission was accomplished had been completed within the first six months. Sometimes God may bring people alongside temporarily, to mentor and support. Some relationships are short-lived, and some are long-term, except for God-ordained covenantal relationships. May God help us discern when the time comes to move on and then enable us to end relationships amicably and respectfully.

For every new season or venture, pray that nothing would hinder your appointment to the right environment. Also, pray that God would bring suitable people, connections, resources, and favor to carry out your assignment.

## God has a Strategy for every Aspect of your Life

God has a plan for everything in your life. But God does not provide a plan without a strategy; He gives information on how the plan will work. Noah received exclusive blueprints for building the ark. God's promise of blessings through Abraham came to pass because he obediently left his home. For Moses, the plan hinged on his sojourn in the desert, his encounter with God, and the specific instructions Moses followed as he led the Israelites out of bondage, later overseeing the building of the Tabernacle. The nation of Israel was born through the obedience of Isaac, Jacob, and Rebecca. Joshua received detailed directives on how to cross the Jordan and take over Jericho, and King Solomon implemented special instructions for the building of the temple.

God loves to be involved in the plans He wants to see accomplished. God has perfect strategies for provision, marriages, families, children, ministry, vocations, businesses, and careers. Since we are God's children, all He has is also ours. Consider it this way; God has a manual for life, and it is our privilege to seek Him for the instructions. God says, *"Call to me, and I will answer you and tell you great and unsearchable things you do not know,"* Jeremiah 33:3, NIV. God invites us to seek Him in the intimate, secret place of devoted prayer. We can find instructions and plans for all areas of life are unknown to us there. Here is a prayer that I have recently begun to pray: "God, give me the blueprint of what You want me to accomplish today, this month and this year."

Successfully carrying out God's plan requires that we fulfill His conditions. Meeting His conditions starts by first submitting our plans, thoughts, and ideas to Him. Proverbs 16:3, ESV advises that we should *"Commit our ways to the Lord, and He will establish them."* When we inquire of the Lord, we can expect an answer. Otherwise, we will suffer the consequences of self-reliance. The Israelites suffered multiple defeats whenever their God-appointed leaders neglected to seek God or follow His commands. We cannot manipulate God to do what we want; neither can we ignore God and assume we will still receive the best outcomes. God has principles and prerequisites that must be met; when God gives them to you, follow every bit of it. Do not omit a word. Consider this warning to Jeremiah, *"thus says the Lord: Stand in the court of the Lord's house, and speak to all the cities of Judah that come to worship in the house of the Lord, all the words that I command you to speak to them; do not hold back a word,"* Jeremiah 26:2, NIV. When we follow God's instructions regardless of any challenges that may arise, outcomes are much more fruitful and favorable to our advantage.

## Right Environment

We have to position ourselves in the proper environment to fulfill God's plans effectively. The word "environment" may apply to a physical location, but also may represent people groups. A wrong setting may cause delay or even failure of the plans God gave us to carry out.

The following are examples of transitions that had to occur to accomplish greater objectives. The transitions involved physical relocations to the place of purpose. Jesus left heaven and came to earth to die for our sins so that He could reconcile humanity to God. Abraham left his family and later had to separate from his cousin, Lot, to receive the promise. Joseph had to be in Egypt to preserve the Israelites. David was promoted from a lowly shepherd to King of Israel and acquired an everlasting kingly inheritance. Transition first starts with a shift in our thinking processes. Once the mind and heart are in alignment, a smooth transition follows in other areas. Transitions pursued in submission to the will of God will result in fruitfulness, growth, expansion, blessings, and accomplishment of God's plans.

At times, God has personally required me, end relationships, shift jobs, or physically relocate leaving possessions behind. The transitions were not always smooth, but nothing is more important than fulfilling God's will. God-directed transitions are for a higher purpose. A transition is a reassignment. The key to a successful transition is to stay sensitive to what God is saying and doing all the time; then you will recognize when God wants you to move. Although change can be difficult, stay open to God. Ask God to give you the grace to navigate the transitions. Ask Him to show you the strategy you need to accomplish for your mission in the new location. Respond quickly to God's directive to move to a new place, but also take time to pray for wisdom to understand the plan. Be assured that, wherever God sends you, He will be there to back you up. You will flourish and do exploits to His glory. Consider this verse, *"everyone who has left houses or brothers or sisters or father or mother or wife or children or fields for my sake will receive a hundred times as much and will inherit eternal life,"* Matthew 19:29, NIV.

Acts, chapter 2, provides an excellent example of how to get in position and prepare for a move of God. Jesus Christ instructed the disciples to go to the upper room and wait for the Holy Spirit. The Lord did not tell them the exact day or time of the outpouring of the Holy Spirit, but they willingly to assembled in the upper room just to wait. They prayed together, fortified with expectancy to see the promise fulfilled. Similarly, positioning ourselves requires obedience and faith. We should align ourselves in anticipation of what God wants to do; being ready for anything at any time. I believe in pursuing a daily, minute-by-minute walk with God. This lifestyle requires us to keep our "channels and frequencies" always open to what God offers. In other words, we should have heightened sensitivity and receptibility to God's voice. I heard a testimony of a man who was prompted by the Holy Spirit to go to a specific shop one morning. He met someone there who later ended up helping him in a significant move to a new vocation. That critical juncture resulted in the establishment of a worldwide ministry that continues to impact many to date. Obedience to a simple instruction, "go to the store," resulted in the expansion of a ministry. This gentleman was in the right place, at the right time, meeting the right person! What an example to mirror!

## God's Timing is the Best

**God also controls the timing of the plans He has for us.** He knows precisely when the time is right to begin or end a task. Therefore, do not be discouraged when you see others advancing faster than you. Throughout the Bible, we see God implementing things at the right time. A critical phrase is "when it came to the fullness of time, God acted." This phrase is very encouraging. Joseph was in Egypt at the right time for the preservation of the nation of Israel. When Joseph died, God later raised Moses to deliver the Israelites. God's promise to Abraham through Isaac came a long time before the nation of Israel was born through Isaac; *"Then He (God) said to Abram: 'Know certainly that your descendants will be strangers in a land that is not theirs and will serve them. They will afflict them four hundred years. And also the nation whom they serve I will judge; afterward, they shall come out with great possessions"* Genesis 15:13-14; NJKV. This is God as the Ancient of Days, the Alpha and Omega, who sees the end from the beginning. Even before Israel became a people, God had already foreseen their deliverance! The same pattern of timely liberation through various leaders is repeated in the book of Judges, culminating in the coming of Jesus Christ.

Be encouraged; God is with you as you implement His plans on earth. You can trust Him with the timing for each plan and the expected outcome. There is no point in trying to rush what God is doing in you, through you, or with you. Stay with the process; premature departure will delay the lesson God wants you to learn, or the promotion He wants to grant you, or the greater purpose He wants you to accomplish. Quitting may also result in repeating the training that God wants you to go through. Endure the process. Peter, the Lord's Apostle and disciple, encouraged us by saying, *"after you have suffered for a little while, the God of all grace, who called you to His eternal glory in Christ, will Himself perfect, confirm, strengthen and establish you,"* 1 Peter 5:10; NASB.

Remember that the Alpha and Omega God is timeless. With God, a day is like a thousand years and a thousand years is like a day, (see 2 Peter 3:8). How delightful to know that God has everything about our life already in place; all we need to do is tag along with Him in close fellowship as He guides us to step into them in perfect timing! See God's guarantee; *"before something happens, I announce how it will end. In fact, from times long ago, I announced what was still to come. I say My plan will succeed. I will do anything I want to do"*, Isaiah 46:10, NIRV.

## Expect to Thrive

Following God's plan produces abundance and overflow. Abraham started with one son but became the father of many nations. Jesus Christ was the one Man crucified for the atonement of the sins of many. Both Abraham and Jesus followed God's plans. This outcome is not measured in material wealth but on a global scale. God desires that we prosper in all things, in life, and godliness, (3 John 1:2). God's intent for Adam and Eve was to be fruitful and multiply; this is my definition of prosperity, wealth, and riches. Since all good things come from God, we should be diligent and productive in our gifts, skills, and vocations. As we submit our ways to God, we can expect God to bless the works of our hands and cause us to flourish. This, again, is a matter of faith; He created us to succeed in all areas of life; that is God's will for us. Cling to God's unique blueprints that He has given you, and you will thrive. Never doubt God's mighty power to work in you and accomplish everything He wants you to do. He will achieve infinitely more than your greatest request, your most unbelievable dream, and exceed your wildest imagination! He will outdo them all, for his miraculous power always energizes you!

# CHAPTER SEVEN

# ABUNDANT LIFE ON EARTH

As I reflected on my life, what I needed was a sense of wholeness. I tried to fill many voids through various means, but only Jesus Christ could satisfy my emptiness! Life without Jesus is empty and devoid of meaning. Satan often attract and deceive people through lies; that offer immediate gratification and are loaded with temporary promises of great things. Satan used this tactic to tempt Jesus, offering Him the kingdoms of this earth if Jesus worshipped him, See Matthew 4:9-11, NIV. Satan must have forgotten that he was tempting his Creator, the Creator of the world, the King of kings! The kind of rewards satan offers are often short-lived, and they lead to destruction. Jesus warns about satan's deception; *"The thief does not come except to steal, and to kill, and to destroy. I have come that they may have life and that they may have it more abundantly,"* John 10:10; NKJV.

From the creation of humanity, God intended to have continuous fellowship with us; thus, humans were created for relationship with God. God also intended humankind to be fruitful and advance in every responsibility. We are enriched by staying in constant fellowship with God, and through the gifts and blessings God provides for each person. God specifies His command to be productive in Genesis 1:26-27. God did not initially design death, sickness, poverty, or fear. Sin brought death to Man; nonetheless, each person can obtain redemption through the blood of Jesus and attain abundant life and prosperity on earth.

## What then, is the meaning of abundant life?

The Merriam dictionary defines [14]abundant as existing or occurring in large amounts, ample, marked by great plenty of resources or amply supplied. Other words for abundance are bounteous or bountiful, generous, and liberal. God's love and thoughts are encapsulated in these descriptions. In God, we can always expect more than enough; in God, we have the assurance that there is no condition too severe for Him to save or rescue. God can heal all types of sickness, and there is no trauma or torment He cannot deliver, and there is no life He cannot restore completely. Job in the Bible is an example of a fellow human being who lost everything, but God later restored him favorably.

Another attribute of the abundant life is eternity. Now, this is a wonderful encouragement. God had already redeemed us from death and destruction, through the blood of Jesus, when we accepted Christ as Lord and Savior. Though we may go through the ups and downs of life, we are guaranteed the hope of eternal life in heaven.

Secondly, we experience abundant life by submitting solely to the Lordship of Jesus Christ and allowing Him to be the source of all that brings joy, security, peace, health, and fulfillment in our lives, because it is in Christ that we live, move and have our being, according to Acts 17:28. Since we are in Him, we can trust God for both our spiritual and material needs. Jesus Christ assures us of His provision, saying, "So *don't worry about these things, saying, 'What will we eat? What will we drink? What will we wear? These things dominate the thoughts of unbelievers, but your heavenly Father already knows all your needs. Seek the Kingdom of God above all else, and live righteously, and he will give you everything you need. So do*

---

[14] Merriam Dictionary

*not worry about tomorrow, for tomorrow will bring its worries. Today's trouble is enough for today,"* Matthew 6:31-34, NLT.

Additionally, life abundant is provided through the fullness of our salvation, with promises of healing, deliverance, and freedom. *"Surely, He has borne our griefs and carried our sorrows; Yet we esteemed Him stricken, smitten by God, and afflicted. But He was wounded for our transgressions; He was bruised for our iniquities; The chastisement for our peace was upon Him, And by His stripes, we are healed"* Isaiah 53:4-5, NKJV. The accounts of His suffering, crucifixion, death, and resurrection attest to the fullness of our salvation. In this fullness, He addresses all areas of our lives, giving us the ability to enjoy and pursue life to the fullest.

Christ took on all aspects of our mental, physical, and emotional pain. The beatings He endured were for our sins. Our redemption covers past, present, and future sins, transgressions, and generational iniquities. Jesus Christ was bruised for our freedom. He endured emotional abuse, verbal insults, mental torture, and pain that we may have peace, and by His stripes, we are healed. This healing pertains to mental, physical, and emotional healing. If we argue that generational curses prevent us from enjoying life in abundance, Christ became a curse on our behalf, breaking every generational curse by His blood at the cross. When curses are broken, we can successfully fulfill the destiny God has for us.

Curses cannot bind us once we renounce and break them because *Christ has rescued us from the curse pronounced by the law. When he was hung on the cross, he took upon himself the curse for our wrongdoing. For it is written in the Scriptures, 'Cursed is everyone who is hung on a tree'",* Galatians 3:13, NLT; Deuteronomy 21:23, NLT. What Christ accomplished at the cross empowers us to break free from every curse, in the Name of Jesus. There is no area of life that is not covered by the sufferings Christ endured for us on the cross; this is abundant life!

Psalm 103 and Psalm 107 are testimonies of my journey into abundant life, the restoration of what satan attempted to steal. I say, "attempted to," because though he tried, he failed. These are Psalms of forgiveness, healing, deliverance, and restoration. In these Psalms, are promises of abundant life provided through God's goodness and mercies that are new each day. Ongoing forgiveness, grace, and immeasurable blessings are not tied to how much I sin or do not sin. My testimony of healing and deliverance starts with, "*Bless the* LORD, *O my soul; and all that is within me, bless His holy name! Bless the* LORD, *O my soul and forget not all His benefits: Who forgives all your iniquities, Who heals all your diseases, Who redeems your life from destruction, Who crowns you with lovingkindness and tender mercies, Who satisfies your mouth with good things, So that your youth is renewed like the eagle's*", Psalm 103:1-3; NKJV. Having abundant life means to be free of sickness, demonic strongholds, and oppression.

Blessings, protection, and breakthroughs resulting from God's goodness towards us are part of the abundant life. God assures us that He will not withhold good things from us (Psalm 84:11). He promises goodness and mercy as a guide each day (Psalm 23:6). God's goodness towards us will never fail; it is plentiful. David declares God's abundant life singing, *how great is the goodness you have stored up for those who fear you, You lavish it on those who come to you for protection, blessing them before the watching world. You hide them in the shelter of your presence safe from those who conspire against them; you shelter them in your presence, far from accusing tongues,*" Psalm 31:19-20; NLT. God is on your side; He is always for you! God wants you to experience abundant life on earth as it is in heaven.

# CHAPTER EIGHT

# GOD WILL RESTORE
# WHAT YOU LOST

I trust that you have done some self-reflection amidst the chapters you have read thus far, and by now, you may be questioning whether there is hope for you. The answer is YES! God often restores out of His bountiful supply of mercy and loving-kindness. His love endures forever, and He will never turn away any child who calls on Him. The Book of Joel highlights God's nature to hold off judgment and His enduring patience as He calls backsliders to repentance and reconciliation with Him. Once reconciled, God promises restoration and recompense for what was lost. Isaiah 61 echoes similar attributes of God's restorative nature. In this chapter, the Prophet Isaiah foretells the ministry of Jesus to comfort and restore what was lost.

> *The Spirit of the Sovereign LORD is on me because the LORD has anointed me to proclaim good news to the poor. He has sent me to bind up the brokenhearted, to proclaim freedom for the captives and release from darkness for the prisoners, to proclaim the year of the LORD's favor and the day of vengeance of our God, to comfort all who mourn, and provide for those who grieve in Zion -to bestow on them a crown of beauty instead of ashes, the oil of joy instead of mourning and a garment of praise instead of a spirit of despair. They will be called oaks of righteousness, a planting of the LORD for the display of his splendor. They will rebuild*

*the ancient ruins and restore the places long devastated; they will renew the ruined cities that have been devastated for generations. Strangers will shepherd your flocks; foreigners will work your fields and vineyards, And you will be called priests of the LORD; you will be named ministers of our God. You will feed on the wealth of nations, and in their riches, you will boast. Instead of your shame, you will receive a double portion, and instead of disgrace, you will rejoice in your inheritance. And so you will inherit a double portion in your land, and everlasting joy will be yours. For I, the LORD, love justice; I hate robbery and wrongdoing. In my faithfulness, I will reward my people and make an everlasting covenant with them. Their descendants will be known among the nations and their offspring among the peoples. All who see them will acknowledge that they are a people the LORD has blessed,"* Isaiah 61:1- 9 NIV.

With these promises in mind, God will meet you right where you are, no matter your condition. A reassuring aspect of Jesus' character is that He loves and welcomes us just as we are. Anyone can respond to God openly, without condemnation. *"He, (God) does not deal with us according to our sins, nor does he punish us according to our iniquities, Psalm 103:10-11, NKJV.* God does not break what is already broken. He does not afflict us because of our sins or failures, and He will not judge us by punishing us still further. He mends us instead. He says that *"A bruised reed he will not break, and a smoldering wick he will not snuff out. In faithfulness, he will bring forth justice"*, Isaiah 42:3, NIV.

God responds to sincere repentance, which is true repentance from the heart, with forgiveness. To repent means to turn away and change the attitude towards sin. Repentance consists of doing a one-eighty degree turn in the opposite direction. This may justify taking some bold steps, such as disconnecting yourself from friends, peers, jobs, or relationships that are ungodly and unhealthy. Repentance may require deleting contact information from cell phones or renouncing destructive habits; these radical steps in the right direction need to be taken immediately; also known as going cold turkey! Some issues may need pastoral guidance, deliverance, or healing of emotional wounds. The Holy Spirit will also help by empowering you to stop harmful habits. God accepts sincere repentance and pays attention to our prayers. The promise is, *"If My people, who are called by my name, will humble themselves and pray and seek my face and turn from their wicked ways, then I will hear from heaven, and I will forgive their sin and will heal their land. Now My eyes will be open, and my ears attentive to the prayers offered in this place,"* 2 Chronicles 7:14-15, NKJV.

After repentance, indulge yourself in prayer and reading the Bible, scheduling regular times for worship. Developing a devotional habit improves intimacy and fellowship with the Holy Spirit, Who will also mentor you in your spiritual life. I cannot overstate the T need to devote to prayer and reading the Bible. Consistency is the key to success in everything, including the time you spend with God. Avoid distractions as much as you can; adjust work schedules, family, or ministry commitments to create that time. Spending time with God also equips you to discern His instructions because they will line up with God's Word. Knowing the Word prevents you from being a victim of evil counsel. By reading the Bible, you will soon authenticate the real truth versus half-truths or false teachings. Ask the Holy Spirit to give you the revelation of what you are about to read before opening the Bible. When you do this. the Holy Spirit will illuminate God's Word to you. Welcome and engage the Holy Spirit and angels in your devotional time. Always ask God and Holy Spirit for direction, discernment, knowledge, and wisdom to proceed on every issue of life. Create time to fellowship with other believers also.

The past is irrelevant when it comes to God's plans for your life: do not dwell on the past. You are free to move on. In God, there is full restoration. The prophet Joel says, *"So I will restore to you the years that the swarming locust has eaten, The crawling locust,*

*The consuming locust, And the chewing locust, My great army which I sent among you. You shall eat in plenty and be satisfied and praise the name of the Lord your God, who has dealt wondrously with you; And My people shall never be put to shame. Then you shall know that I am amid Israel. I am the Lord your God, and there is no other. My people shall never be put to shame", Joel 2:25-27, NKJV.*

If you feel that you lost time, resources, or relationships, know that God will restore those. There are possessions you may have to discard, and there are relationships you may need to end, out of obedience to God. Despite what the enemy stole or destroyed, be assured, like Job, that God will restore it. God will turn and use what the enemy meant for evil for your good.

We are currently in a season of uncertainty due to the major medical crisis occurring throughout the world. Global economies have been affected, businesses have suffered significant losses, and many people are unemployed due to layoffs. Nevertheless, God remains faithful. He is not anxious or overwhelmed by what is happening. He still promises restoration for the righteous, both spiritually and materially. God restored Job with a double portion of possessions and a double portion of children, following his season of adversity. *"And the Lord restored Job's losses when he prayed for his friends. Indeed, the Lord gave Job twice as much as he had before. After this, Job lived one hundred and forty years and saw his children and grandchildren for four generations", Job 42:10,16, NKJV.* Job's suffering mirrors what is happening in the world today, where all sectors of our lives are affected. However, as God provided for Job, He will also provide for us.

God's plans are always greater than disappointments! As you petition God for your needs, be confident that your prayers are not in vain. God honors and responds to the prayers of the righteous. Talk to God about everything that you have lost. Ask Him to restore or replace anything that is barren, broken, destroyed, or stolen. God will restore you, and you will be more fruitful and make more of an impact than before.

# CHAPTER NINE

# EMBRACE YOUR NEW IDENTITY

Every year the Lord takes me through a journey to discover something new. However, before exposing the revelation, God often takes me through a period of purging, healing, releasing the past, forgiving, deliverance, rest, peace, and joy; then, He shares the new revelation. In 2017, the Lord began to introduce me to my true identity, showing me where I belonged and how He values me.

The path that led to my true identity started with a purging process that God used to reveal deep-seated false beliefs and the negative mindsets I had developed. The cleansing process revealed the source of my fears and highlighted areas where I felt inadequate. Some of that included negative perception of my physical appearance and what some people thought about me. There were some hurts I blamed myself for, along with rebellion, self-sabotage, self-reliance, and self-preservation. The Lord also taught me that the root of so many problems is fear and loss of identity.

The Lord continued to teach me that if I would learn my true identity in Him:

- I would not be shaken by what I did or did not do. This realization involved having a sense of confidence even when I made mistakes

- I could comfortably be my genuine self, unaffected by other people's opinions, judgments, or criticism

- I would know what belongs to me and the purpose of pursuing it.

- I would not compete with others, compare myself to others, or covet what belongs to another

- I would know and exert the authority and exercise the power I have in Jesus Christ

- I would use what I have and be effective, fruitful, and productive in it

- I would approach God boldly, yet reverently; I would be at ease and relate with Him freely as friends relate to one another or as a child relates to a loving parent

The Lord revealed three areas that played a part in the loss of identity. These were specific to me, but they may vary from person to person.

First, we lose our identity when we shift our focus away from our Maker, Who gave us individuality and designed us with a purpose in mind. When we lose sight of that purpose or plan, we labor under a false identity and a misguided destiny. God's intentions towards us reflect in the destinies of Prophet Jeremiah and King David. God affirmed Jeremiah's calling and destiny, saying, *"before I formed you in the womb and I knew you before you were born I set you apart; I appointed you as a prophet to the nations,"* Jeremiah 1:5, NKJV. King David, in his writings, was aware of this predestination, saying, *"You created every part of me; you put me together in my mother's womb. I praise you because you are to be feared; all you do is strange and wonderful. I know it with all my heart. When my bones were being formed, carefully put together in my mother's womb, when I was growing there in secret, you knew that I was there— you saw me before I was born".* Psalm 139:13-14, GNT. It is reassuring to know that each of us was predestined-God knew us and our destinies planned way before we were born. All we need to do now is to walk in the blueprints of those plans.

Secondly, we lose our identity when we are not convinced of God's love for us. In the previous chapters, I discussed the lack of affection in my childhood and the rejection I experienced afterward. These unmet needs, coupled with fatherlessness and my quest to beat the odds, distorted my view of God as a loving Father. I felt like God was always mad at me for "something"; some indefinable, unattainable reason. But God revealed His love for me through Scripture in Jeremiah and affirmed my restoration and ability to receive His love. God describes this endless love as, *"I have loved you with an everlasting love; Therefore, with lovingkindness, I have drawn you. Again I will build you, and you shall be rebuilt, O virgin of Israel! You shall again be adorned with your tambourines and shall go forth in the dances of those who rejoice",* Jeremiah 31:3-4, NKJV. In addition to God's love, these Scriptures also affirm the restoration of Israel's identity and purpose. Just as the Lord restored the nation of Israel to her true identity, God will restore yours as well!

Third, we lose our identity when we think we are inadequate. These attitudes can manifest in feeling insufficient, unqualified, or ill-equipped. Consequently, we do not take risks or try new things, we remain stagnant by resisting change, and we settle for less due to the stronghold of inadequacy, yet God is not unaware of our plight.

God knows our inadequacies. He does not define us by them, nor let our shortcomings withhold us from accomplishing His purposes. Genesis 1:27 outlines our creation: God created humanity as male and female, in the image of God, but that is not limited to a reflection of our physical features. This image encompasses how God thinks, sees, and works, and involves viewing life from God's perspective. In a nutshell, how God sees us, and what He intends for us is of great importance, regardless of our faults.

When God called Moses to rescue the Israelites, the story highlights the assurance that God will use us despite our weaknesses; God knows them all, yet He still uses us to fulfill His plan. When God first approached Moses with an assignment, Moses' response to God was that he was not qualified for the job. He said he was not a great orator because he stuttered. Here is the account of their exchange:

> Moses said to the LORD, 'Pardon your servant, Lord. I have never been eloquent, neither in the past nor since you have spoken to your servant. I am slow of speech and tongue.' The LORD said to him, 'Who gave human beings their mouths? Who makes them deaf or mute? Who gives them sight or makes them blind? Is it not I, the LORD? Now go; I will help you speak and will teach you what to say'. But Moses said, 'Pardon your servant, Lord. Please send someone else.' Then the LORD's anger burned against Moses, and he said, 'What about your brother, Aaron the Levite? I know he can speak well. He is already on his way to meet you, and he will be glad to see you. You shall speak to him and put words in his mouth; I will help both of you speak and will teach you what to do. He will speak to the people for you, and it will be as if he were your mouth and as if you were God to him. But take this staff in your hand so you can perform the signs with it," Exodus 4:10-17, NIV.

The discussion above gives us strategies for overcoming our inadequacies, based on the response that God gave Moses. First, When we know who we are, we can be transparent with God, in Whose image we are created. Psalm 139 tells us that everything in us is visible to God. He knows our strengths and weaknesses and yet still considers us to be fearfully and wonderfully made. Accepting this statement allows us to relate to God freely without trying to be something that we are not. We should not focus on our weaknesses, but we can acknowledge them, knowing they will not interfere with God's plans. Secondly, be aware that God will use both our shortcomings and our strengths for the good of His plans and purposes; (see Romans 8.28). God also promises to bring everything which concerns us to fruition;(see Psalm 138:8). Thirdly, God will provide a support system to complement our inadequacies, achieve His goals, and accomplish our destiny. As with Moses' assignment, God ensured that Moses had a support system in place. God appointed Aaron to support Moses, and God also supplied Moses with a rod to perform the work that was required. Our skills, talents, gifts, and abilities comprise our "rod." God will use them and give additional tools to fulfill our assignment.

Every spiritual gift, natural gift, skill, or talent was given by God to solve a problem. No gift or skill is too small. There is a problem somewhere waiting for your expertise. Do not minimize yourself, do not sell yourself short. God has anointed that very gift, talent, and skill to solve a problem. Trust the Holy Spirit to infuse your skill with, His breath of wisdom, knowledge, understanding. Remember God has a habit of multiplying exceedingly small things. Just step out! (see Exodus 31: 1-6, 1 Kings 7:13-14)

If you have ever lost something valuable and then recovered it, you can relate to chapter 31 in Exodus. God rejoices in our restoration. No matter how far we have walked away from God, His restorative nature aims to bring you back to what He created you to be. God takes pleasure in the success and accomplishment of His children. This reason is part of why Jesus Christ died for us; that we who were far off should be reconciled to fellowship with Him and come to fullness of identity in Him, (see Ephesians 2:17).

The initial process discussed in the previous chapter comprised the first steps to my complete restoration in Jesus Christ. Before discovering my true identity, I chased after academia, career, and perfectionism to define who I was. I also craved security, affirmation, and love– all of these led to compromise, as I lowered my standards to feed my false identity. These were self-defeating, self-destructive paths! I felt empty and void of meaning, and in time, I realized that "I had lost me."

Our identity is in Christ, and our identity remains rooted in Him, not in the standards of this world through false rewards of accolades or possessions. Our abilities do not define us, nor economic or social status, job titles, or family backgrounds. Our unique identity is who God created us to be, our permanent and irreplaceable personhood. WHAT God created us to do is our DESTINY. Identity and destiny go hand in hand; we cannot do what we were assigned to do if we do not know who we are. My self-driven quest for success apart from God resulted in an identity crisis, so I said, "I lost me." I can argue that I had legitimate reasons for arriving there, but, over time and through inner healing, I realized I was misdirected by my false ideas of who I was. Through deliverance, prayer, fasting, reading the Bible, and listening to sound teaching, the Holy Spirit began redirecting me to my true identity. This process has taken a while, and the journey is ongoing, but rediscovering myself feels great!

The other lesson on identity came as I was preparing for a mission trip. One of the ways the Holy Spirit mentors me is by getting me interested in a subject; to learn about it, and then present it to others. My initial study on identity began in 2018; when God directed me to prepare messages for a mission trip to high school students in Africa. Since I had just started to discover the impact of false identity, I studied the powerful effect of healthy, real identity. This topic was much-needed for teenagers, who can be unsure of their individuality. I can gladly sing of God's amazing grace- that I once was lost, but now I am found because I know who I am. Knowledge of our identity is essential. The following are excerpts from my notes for the mission trip:

- **Identity provides direction.** When I know who I am, I can more confidently follow God's directives to fulfill my destiny, even when that direction is not what everyone else is doing.

- **Knowledge of destiny activates focus.** If I do not know who I am, I might get sidetracked by deceptive beliefs or actions that are not related to my destiny. This confusion could cause uncertainty and result in frustration, lack of productivity, self-reliance, self-preservation, and missed opportunities.

- **Our Identity in Christ grants authority.** My authority is contingent on my secure understanding of who I am. I can operate effectively in great authority and power that Jesus Christ has bestowed on me to carry out God's plans for my life.

- **Exceptional ability to appropriately steward gifts and skills** -There are no mediocre or unworthy skills, gifts, or professions in the kingdom of God. When I know my identity, I can accurately channel my giftings in alignment with my destiny. Gifts propel destiny.

- **Knowing one's identity boosts morale and confidence.** We can pursue plans for life with the confidence that comes from God. The book of Joshua outlines Caleb's confidence in asking Joshua for his inheritance and acquiring it. At eighty years old, Caleb was confident that he could fight for and gain Mount Hebron. Caleb said ... "so here I am today, eighty-five years old! I am still as strong today as the day Moses sent me out; I'm just as vigorous to go out to battle now as I was then," Joshua 14:10-13, NIV Caleb was a one-of-a-kind mand who was confident in God's strength to go for his portion of the promised land at eighty years old. We, too, can at any stage of our lives go after what belongs to us because we know Whose we are and who we are!

## Be Comfortable With Yourself

We are unique creations of God with various abilities to serve and support humanity. Everyone has something to offer. Contained in each human being is an exceptional treasure, despite external faults that often seem magnified. Despite our modern society's view of what constitutes our identity such as what we do or what we have, boldly embrace the identity God has given you. Cherish your individuality; be comfortable in your skin. Your calling and life assignments are specific to you. God wants you to excel in life and be prosperous.

The subject of identity is vast. However, it is comforting to know that accepting Jesus as Lord and Savior, changes our identity to reflect His nature. We are predestined, chosen vessels, called to holiness. Though still on earth, we are all kings and priests who reign with Jesus Christ and have the authority to influence supernatural and natural spheres. We are co-heirs with Christ Jesus, sons, and daughters, who have been adopted into a kingdom with a rich inheritance.

You must be comfortable and courageous in your new identity, because some people who knew your past life may try to relate with you in that old identity. Such people will try to bring up your past in conversations, often in public. Be bold and remind them that you are no longer operating from that identity. Resist invitations and temptations to linger in the company of such people. Stay in the company of encouragers and people who will mentor you and advance your new journey. Be prepared, however, to show love still to those who may never embrace you. Continue to live your life righteously; your light will eventually win them. That said, you are not obligated to defend yourself or try to prove that you are no longer living in your previous sinful nature. The fruit of your life will speak for itself. Light always overpowers darkness! Keep your head up and continue to go after God with all your heart!

According to Psalm 139:14, each human being is fearfully and wonderfully made. That wonderfulness applies not only to outward appearance but to our gifts, vocations, and potential. Christ has given us a new identity which reflects adoption as sons and daughters of the Most High God. We are a royal priesthood, a peculiar people, friends of God, chosen and set apart for Him. Greater is He that is in us than he that is in the world, and we are more than conquerors in Christ Jesus. We are called to and endowed for exploits. We are valuable treasures per God's standards. We are the apple of God's eyes. This is our identity!

Consider this promise: *"the glory of this present house will be greater than the glory of the former house,' says the LORD Almighty. And in this place, I will grant peace,' declares the LORD Almighty"*, *Haggai 2:9, NIV.* We are God's children. With the Holy Spirit as a guarantee, we can live to our fullest potential, knowing that God will never forsake us in this journey. God wants each of us to succeed; this is part of our identity and inheritance as His children. Through the Holy Spirit, God can help you rediscover yourself. The Holy Spirit will reignite your passion for God and activate your gifts. You will come out much more robust, and wiser, in your restored identity. Your latter glory shall be greater than the former. This is the promise of a restored identity!

# CHAPTER TEN

# INVITATION TO CHOOSE GOD'S PLAN FOR YOUR LIFE

My reasons for seeking my plan were many, as you have already read, but to sum them up: I wanted to be in control of my life! My zeal for control my life resulted in self-reliance, self-preservation, frustration, and discontentment. I was also pursuing a life apart from my true identity. Nonetheless, God, in His mercy and love, still drew me back to Him. I was the one sheep out of ninety-nine that He could not let go. Why? Because I was predestined to be His before I was even born!

God thinks highly of you too, and He is ready to rescue one out of many. If you can relate to any portion of this book, I know that God wants to restore you to His original plan. God has not changed His mind about that plan. He is only waiting for you to respond to Him. There is only one way to access that plan, and it is through Jesus Christ. Jesus said, *"I am the way, the truth, and the life. No one comes to the Father except through me"*, John 14:6, NKJV. God also desires that you live life to the fullest, here on earth, before you transition to heaven. This abundant life is also guaranteed to your children and future generations if they choose Jesus as the Way. God says, *"See, I have set before you today life and good, death and evil. I call heaven and earth as witnesses today against you, that I have set before your life and death, blessing, and cursing; therefore choose life, that both you and your descendants may live"*, Deuteronomy 30:15, 19 NKJV.

The first step in determining God's plan for your life is to acknowledge Him through salvation and submit to His guidance. Salvation is obtained by accepting Jesus Christ as your Lord and Savior. Believe that He was crucified, died, and rose again for your redemption. This is a faith-empowered statement or prayer that you can make to invite Jesus into your life. The Apostle Paul says, *"if you confess with your mouth the Lord Jesus and believe in your heart that God raised Him from the dead, you will be saved,"* Romans 10:9, NKJV. Following this prayer, invite the Holy Spirit into your life. The Holy Spirit will teach and guide you in your new life as a believer. Please see the last page of this book for the prayer of salvation and invitation of the Holy Spirit.

One of the most notable attributes of our God is that He does not deal with us based on our past histories or sins. He is a Just God, one who shows no favoritism; He is not a respecter of persons. He is the God whose character remains unchallenged to the just and unjust (see Matthew 5:45). God accepts us as we are. God will use our weaknesses, opportunities, and strengths to all work for our good (Romans 8:28). Come to Him as you are and allow the Holy Spirit to work through your personality traits, physical appearance, character, speech, gifts, talents, home, and finances; I mean everything. Be yourself! I encourage you to submit to the Holy Spirit and allow Him to lead you. Give the Holy Spirit full access to all areas of your life. As you submit to the Holy Spirit, He will mold and transform you gradually to the image of God, *"now the Lord is the Spirit; and where the Spirit of the Lord is, there is liberty. But we all, with unveiled face, beholding as in a mirror the glory of the Lord, are being transformed into the same image from glory to glory, just as by the Spirit of the Lord"*, 2 Corinthians 3:17-18; NKJV

Once you have surrendered to the leadership of the Holy Spirit, be diligent in following His directions and, most importantly, understand that God's blessings are conditional to our obedience. Obeying the Holy Spirit is key to success in life. So, it behooves us to understand the conditions God has placed for success in all areas of life. The writer of 1 Samuel emphasizes that, *"obedience is better than sacrifice,"* 1 Samuel 15:22 NKJV. God's blessings are crucially linked to following His commands, (see Deuteronomy 28:1-14, NKJV).

Obviously, God's plans were different from mine. I believe that God has strategies and timelines for each objective he has planned for us. God knows the conditions and environments these plans will thrive in and the resources, support systems, and people to bring success to His plans. Remember also that since we were predestined, God's plans also preexisted before our birth. God desires to guide us successfully in every area of our life. This is the promise in which God assures us," *I will instruct you and teach you in the way you should go; I will guide you with My eye," Psalm 32:8 NKJV.* I believe that God celebrates our successes and loves to see us thrive. God wants us to live accomplished lives because He is the initiator of everything we do, and He promises to see us through it all. We can succeed in all areas of life by following God's ways without compromise or seeking ungodly alternatives.

The restoration process may be long, but the undertaking is worth the time; however, all will not be restored immediately. Some areas may require preparation to accommodate the blessings that will be coming our way. I discovered that such preparation was tied to emotional healing or deliverance. We need to heal from the wounds of betrayal, rejection, unforgiveness, and bitterness. The path of restoration typically involves an internal purging before the manifestation of the physical blessings- this was my case. I believe God does this because we may unknowingly dismiss or despise His blessings. The environments they land in, primarily our hearts, may not be ready. So God takes us through the process of healing and deliverance, a cleansing of sorts to make room for blessings.

Allow God to do a thorough emotional, and spiritual house-cleaning, regardless of how painful your experiences were.

Recently, while studying the book of Daniel, I noticed a pattern: a promotion always followed each adversity that Daniel, Meshach, Shadrack, and Abednego faced. In their case, they were granted governmental promotions, or, in today's terms, executive political promotions, see the first six chapters of Daniel. From the study, I concluded that God never forsakes the righteous. These four believers were bold and adamant, they stood their ground, and they were unwilling to compromise God's commands, even if it cost them their lives. They exemplify the latter part of Revelation, which says *they did not love their lives to the death," Revelation 12:11b NKJV.* Daniel, Meshach, Shadrack, and Abednego were confident that God would deliver them, and God did! I have added their story here to encourage you. Some tests may come because you have now recommitted your life to live for God wholeheartedly. Endure the adversities should they come; the Lord considers us worthy and blessed when we successfully overcome them. We, too, will have a greater reward in heaven (Matthew 5:10-11). Also, expect to be rewarded while still alive on earth. God may reward and promote us in different ways, although they may not necessarily be monetary incentives. However, I believe that as we endure in righteousness, the promotion will be higher than what we had before, and better than the place where we were previously.

God's plans for you have not changed! He desires that you fulfill your destiny and accomplish it well. Reflect on this thought frequently, *"do not remember the former things, nor consider the things of old. Behold, I will do a new thing; now it shall spring forth. Shall you not know it? I will even make a road in the wilderness and rivers in the desert,"* Isaiah 43:18-19, NKJV. So do your best to stay focused, forgetting the past, because this latter phase is better. God does not restore the old; instead, He replaces what was lost with better and greater things!

In closing, trust God that all things have worked for good and will continue working in your favor because you are called according to God's purpose. This means that God can bring good from harmful things, too. God does not afflict us with trials (James 1:12-15), but He allows them when we rebel. He tests us to check our hearts, discipline, teach, and mature us. I often reflect on the thought that **all things** work for good. The writer of Psalm 119 acclaimed God's goodness despite his afflictions, saying, *"You have dealt well with your servant, O Lord, according to your word. Teach me good judgment and knowledge, for I believe in your commandments. Before I was afflicted, I went astray, but now I keep your word. You are good and do good; teach me your statutes, Psalm 119:65-68, ESV.* I, too, testify that God has worked everything for my good, including the consequences of my choices, unsolicited adversities, and chastening of the Lord. Everything will work for your good also. As you return to God, the Lord Himself will, in turn, perfect, strengthen, establish you; and lead you through to the successful completion of your destiny! If God can do it for me, He can redirect you back to the plans He intended for you. This is my testimony, a restored backslider!

# CHAPTER ELEVEN

## PRAYERS TO RENOUNCE SELF-RELIANCE

While reviewing my journal, I came across prayers that I frequently use to renounce self-reliance. As someone who had been independent and analytical for so long, occasionally, I still catch myself wanting to take control and make independent decisions without consulting the Holy Spirit. I prayed the following prayer initially when God exposed the sin of self-reliance to me. Consider using it as a guide. I believe in utilizing Scriptures in prayer; the accompanying Scriptures are related to surrendering everything to God and submitting to the Lordship of Jesus Christ.

Proverbs 3:5-6, ESV: Trust in the Lord with all your heart and do not lean on your own understanding. In all your ways, acknowledge him, and he will make straight your path or direct your paths. The key prayer strategy and declaration is to *commit your plans, decisions, dreams, ideas, and goals to the Lord, and He will establish them.*

Proverbs 32:8-9, NKJV: I will instruct you and teach you in the way you should go; I will guide you with My eye. Do not be like the horse or like the mule, which have no understanding, which must be harnessed with bit and bridle; else they will not come near you. The prayer strategy and declaration from these verses are that *the Lord will guide you in all areas of your life.*

Isaiah 41:10 NKJV: Fear not, for I am with you; Be not dismayed, for I am your God. I will strengthen you, Yes, I will help you, I will uphold you with My righteous right hand.' The prayer approach and declaration are *that God is with you, pursue your destiny confidently without fear because God will be with you.*

## Prayer to Renounce Self-Reliance

*Father in the Name of Jesus, I thank you for the redemption Jesus Christ has provided me through His death on the Cross. I thank you that the Blood of Jesus justifies me. Therefore I repent of all decisions that I have made independently without asking you, Lord. I repent for not consulting the Holy Spirit before taking any action; I repent of ignoring His instructions and for disobeying the Holy Spirit. Holy Spirit, I ask that you expose every area of rebellion, stubbornness, independence, and self-will. Lord, I repent of relying on my intellect, knowledge, resources, people, and for depending on my abilities to run my life. Forgive me, Lord. I receive your forgiveness in Jesus' Name.*

*Father in the Name of Jesus and by the Blood of Jesus Christ, I break every legal right to operate in my life that I granted Satan knowingly or unknowingly. I break evil covenants and vows established due to my self-reliance in Jesus' Name. I command all demons, familiar spirits, and every evil influence associated with self-reliance operating in my life to leave my life right now in Jesus' Name. I command every evil operation to cease, all soul-ties with evil entities be broken right now in Jesus' Name. Father in the Name of Jesus, I close every evil gate that may have been opened by the sin of self-reliance in Jesus' Name.*

*In the Name of Jesus Christ, I break all curses related to self-sufficiency in my life by the Blood of Jesus. I break cycles of bad decisions in Jesus' Name; I break demonic alliances of robbery, waste, extortion, and swindling. I break every evil covenant and curse operating in my life; I break the curses of depression, worry, loneliness, and self-reliance in Jesus' Name. I break them off and declare them powerless over my life. I break helplessness. I cast out every spirit of control, manipulation, jealousy, envy, and bitterness; I cast out every spirit of deception in Jesus' Name. I subdue and break principalities, powers, witches, warlocks, word curses, and cancel the effects of persons conjuring and planning evil against my life in Jesus' Name. Lord thwart their plans and agenda in Jesus' Name. Holy Spirit, I submit to You, I receive Your anointing, power, grace, and favor to live a successful goldy life in Jesus' Name, Amen.*

## Prayer to Submit to the Lordship of Jesus Christ

It is vital to depend entirely on God; this requires surrendering every aspect of our lives to God, including the decisions we make and the actions we take. Here is a prayer of submission: Father in the Name of Jesus I submit to you as The Almighty God and my Father. Lord Jesus, I submit to you not only as my Savior but as my Lord. Holy Spirit, I submit to you as my helper, guide, comforter, advocate, intercessor, and the source of my strength and wisdom in all things. I ask Lord that you guide and lead me according to Your Word. I ask Lord that you release anything that was withheld due to my self-reliance and reopen the doors of blessings. I declare that I am Your child and I am blessed with spiritual and natural blessings in Christ the Lord, Amen

## The Prayer of Salvation and the Baptism of the Holy Spirit

Only Jesus Christ can make us complete. This book is about trying to seek fulfillment and purpose for life, apart from God, and experiencing the restorative power of God's love. Jesus Christ is the Key through Whom we gain access to God. We cannot know God without knowing Jesus. Jesus shares this assurance, *"I am the way, the truth, and the life. No one can come to the Father except through Me"*, **John 14:6, NIV.** Accepting Jesus Christ as your Lord and Savior will grant you access to start enjoying the fullness of God.

Jesus died for our redemption, deliverance, and healing. As stated in the book of Isaiah, *"He (Jesus) was wounded for our transgressions, He was bruised for our iniquities; the chastisement for our peace was upon Him, and by His stripes, we are healed,"* **Isaiah 53:5, NKJV**. Invite Jesus Christ into your life by praying out loud the prayer below:

> *Dear God, I come to You. I accept your Son, Jesus Christ, as my Lord and Savior. I believe that Jesus died and rose again for my sins so that I may receive salvation. I, therefore, repent of my sins, transgressions, and iniquities, and I ask for Your forgiveness. I renounce sin and all forms of wickedness. I renounce all gods that I have served, vowed to, submitted to, or that I ever made sacrifices to them. Lord Jesus, now come into my life and into everything that concerns me. Come in, Lord Jesus, and be Lord over my life and align me to the path and plan you have for me. In the name of Jesus Christ, I pray. Amen.*

Now invite the Holy Spirit who will help, teach, and guide you in this new life. You can pray:

> Holy Spirit, I now welcome You. Come to reside in me and take over every aspect of my life. I submit to You, Holy Spirit, guide me in knowledge, wisdom, revelation, discernment, and counsel to walk and accomplish the plan God has for me. Holy Spirit fill me with Your gifts that I may be exceedingly productive in the name of Jesus, I pray. Amen!

If you have sincerely prayed the prayer above, with all your heart, then welcome to God's family! You are now a child of God who is clothed in righteousness. Christ is currently living in you, and His power, love, and glory are operating in you through the Holy Spirit. This is my prayer for you:

*In the Mighty Name of Jesus, and by the blood of the Lamb, I command you to be delivered from any bondage of Satan. I rebuke, flush out, and expel any demonic occupant in your life, your bloodline, and your body. I loose you from every bondage of Satan. You are now set free by the blood of the Lamb. Receive your healing. Receive your deliverance.*

*I command your mind to be restored, in the Mighty Name of Jesus. Receive restoration and restitution. I command permanency of the good things God has started in you. I decree your fruitfulness, multiplication, sustainability, and longevity in everything God has for you, according to His perfect will and plan, in the Mighty Name of Jesus! Amen! And Amen!*

Next, please purchase a Bible with space on the page to write notes, in a version that you can easily understand, such as NLT, NJKV, or ESV translations. Start by reading the Gospel of John; then read the book of Proverbs, then the New Testament from Matthew to Revelation, read the rest of the Bible beginning from Genesis. Try reading a chapter in the morning and another one at night before bedtime, followed by prayer. Do this regularly. Also, find a church to attend that believes in the power and gifts of the Holy Spirit. Let the pastor know that you recently accepted Jesus as your Savior; ask them to baptize you by immersion in water. Then ask the pastor to direct you on how to be discipled. The Holy Spirit will also teach and disciple you; just ask Him. Welcome to God's Kingdom!

# OTHER BOOKS BY PAULINE

**Praying the Names and Attributes of God**-*Receive extraordinary outcomes when you partner with God in prayer when you apply His Names and attributes in Prayer -Synergy with the Trinity in prayer*

**Victorious Overcomer Prayers and Declarations for Spiritual Warfare**- *Declarations and Prayers for Spiritual Warfare-Manual: Prayers to break demonic covenants, rituals, dedications, thrones, witchcraft, and altars*

**Vencedor Victorioso -Declaraciones y oraciones para la guerra espíritu.** *(Spanish Version)-Declaraciones y oraciones para la guerra espíritu. Oraciones para romper pactos demoniacos, convenios, dedicaciones, rituales, altares, tronos, maldiciones y brujería.*

**Dreams and Encounter Journal**- *A journal with instructions of how to follow through on dreams and encounters*

**Familiarity** -*Ways in which we can miss God based on an attitude of familiarity -How satan deceives through familiarity*

**Prayer is Simply Talking to God**- *(Book and accompanying CD)- Everyone can pray effectively, simple steps to jump-start your prayer life, and receive answers. Prayer is two-way communication with God*

**Ministry Beyond the Pulpit**- *Not everyone is called to the platform. How to use your gifts to influence where God has placed you*

**Called to Ministry Now What***! - How to recognize your calling, what to do and how to navigate your encounters with God*

**The Alternative Plan-1ˢᵗ Edition***- Pauline's testimony of how God restored her life to align with His intended Plan*

Books and other Merchandise can be
purchased at www.paulineadongo.com

Printed in the United States
By Bookmasters